HISTORIC DEKALB COUNTY

An Illustrated History

By Vivian Price

Commissioned by the DeKalb History Center

Historical Publishing Network
A division of Lammert Incorporated
San Antonio, Texas

Contents

ISBN: 9781893619890

Library of Congress Card Catalog Number: 2008935124

Historic DeKalb County: An Illustrated History

author: Vivian Price

cover artist: Maceo Rogers

contributing writers for "Sharing the Heritage": Brenda Thompson
Britt Fayssoux

Historical Publishing Network

president: Ron Lammert

project manager: Violet Caren

administration: Donna M. Mata
Melissa Quinn

book sales: Dee Steidle

production: Colin Hart
Craig Mitchell
Chuck Newton
Evelyn Hart
Joshua Johnston
Roy Arellano

DeKalb History Center

Presidents

1947 – 2008

1947	Carl Hudgins
1948 - 1949	Julius McCurdy
1950 – 1952	Mrs. Hugh H. Trotti
1953	J. Calvin Weaver
1954	W. Bayne Gibson
1955 – 1956	David H. Ansley
1957	Faye H. Robarts
1958 – 1959	Percy Plant
1960	George W. Jacobs
1961 – 1962	Roy A. Grizzell
1963	Thomas Carlton Carter
1964	Roscoe Snead
1965	Hugh H. Howell, Jr.
1966 – 1967	B. F. (Bennie) Wilkins
1968 – 1969	Walter P. McCurdy, Jr.
1970	Charles L. Davidson, Jr.
1971 – 1972	William C. Thibadeau
1973 – 1974	Otis & Jane Norcross
1975	Ernie Ramsey
1976 – 1979	Jim Cherry
1980 – 1981	Jim Miller
1982 – 1984	Peggy Hill Thompson Sims
1985 – 1987	James A. Mackay
1988 – 1989	Curtis James
1990	Bill Roth
1991	Claire Johnson
1992 – 1994	Lyn Menne
1995	Charlotte Rife Rowell
1996	Robert L. Brown
1997	Jimmy Dickey
1998	Scott Candler, III
1999	Cynthia Alford
2000	David Purcell
2001	Betty Willis
2002	Dr. James Reynolds Hallford
2003	Darro Willey
2004	Julia Fare
2005	Jon D. Manns/Sue Ellen Williams
2006	Jack Regan
2007	Jon D. Manns
2008	Scott Candler, III

Executive Directors

1976 - 1980	Gordon M. Midgette
1980 – 1987	Dorothy Nix
1988 – 1991	Bob Kothe
1992 – 2007	Sue Ellen Williams
2007 - Present	Melissa Forgey

2008 Board of Directors

President	Scotty Candler
Treasurer	Robert W. Espy, IV
Past President	Jack Regan
President Elect	Stuart M. Zola, Ph.D.
Secretary	Cherie Bennett

Melvin Bettis
Frank Burdette
Jane Grabowski
Lynn Cherry Grant
Mary K. Jarboe
Kathryn Johnson
John Keys
Jon D. Manns
Albert Martin
Kerri Morrin
Elizabeth M. Roberts
Paula S. Swartzberg
Helen Talley-McRae
Kenneth H. Thomas, Jr.
Johnny Waits, Jr.
Dr. Eugene P. Walker

Through the Years

✧

DeKalb County was named for Baron Johann DeKalb, a hero of the American Revolution. A native Bavaria, he died in 1780 from wounds received in the Battle of Camden, South Carolina. DeKalb citizens contributed to a monument at the site, which was dedicated in 1825.

Forty years after the end of the American Revolution, citizens were confident, on the move, and in a patriotic mood. Georgia's land lotteries made the state irresistible. Henry County, named for American patriot Patrick Henry, had been created in 1821 from land given up by the Creek Indians. Henry was divided by the Georgia legislature to create the state's fify-fourth county on December 9, 1822.

The new jurisdiction was named for an American Revolutionary hero, Johann DeKalb, a Bavarian peasant who by his hard work and courageous fighting on behalf of the American cause earned himself the title of baron.

The new county was much larger than it is today—stretching from Stone Mountain to the Chattahoochee River.

Setters in the new county were greeted by a sea of trees and abundant creeks. Indians introduced settlers to new agricultural practices, foodstuffs, and herbal medicines. Doctors like Chapmon Powell treated Indians and whites and traded gold to the Cherokees for herbs. Cherokees lived with the Dempsey Perkerson family on land along the South River. Indians are said to have helped build the Solomon Goodwin house on Peachtree Road.

Indian trails became the beds for today's highways and railways. The Etowah (Hightower) Trail became the county's eastern border. DeKalb's oldest and least changed Indian trail runs up the western slope of Stone Mountain.

Where Creek, Cherokee, and later white territory converged were two Indian settlements along the Chattahoochee River. One, by the name of Standing Peachtree, was located where Peachtree Creek flows into the great river. The other, called Buzzard's Roost and (later Sandtown) settlement, was located at the junction of Utoy Creek and the river in what is now southwest Fulton County.

At the time of the county's organization, a few hearty souls already had settled in the territory, most notably the family of James McConnell Montgomery. Coming as most DeKalb settlers did from the Carolinas by way of east Georgia counties, the Montgomerys set the standard not only for pioneering spirit, but also for contributions to the community. James Montgomery was the first to serve in many of DeKalb's first public jobs, including census taker. From 1828 to 1832 much of the formerly Cherokee Indian land belonged to DeKalb, giving Montgomery a huge territory for the county's first federal census in 1830. Probably half of the 10,047 people Montgomery counted lived north of the Chattahoochee River.

The place that would become Decatur, the official seat of the new county, began as a trading post at the intersection of two Indian trails. The town of Decatur was incorporated by the Georgia legislature on December 10, 1823, named for U.S. Naval hero Stephen Decatur. From its humble beginnings, the town quickly grew to a population of thirty-five hundred.

One of the first orders of business was setting aside land for a cemetery. Decatur Cemetery is the last resting place for the city's prominent citizens from politicians to pastors to poets. The oldest known birth date in the cemetery belongs to Ann Reynolds, wife of Francis Reynolds, who was born on April 28, 1750, and died on February 16, 1827.

The cemetery was the scene of a skirmish that was part of the Civil War Battle of Atlanta on July 22, 1864, and some 124 Confederate soldiers killed in the fighting are buried throughout the cemetery. The styles of markers in the cemetery vary from rough fieldstone to ornate Victorian cemetery art.

Decatur also was the site of the county's first school, the DeKalb Academy, started in 1825. Although the concept of free, public education began to be discussed in the 1850s, the county's first public schools—grades one through eight—did not open until 1873. Public high schools did not exist until 1910.

The discovery of gold in north Georgia in 1829 spread "gold fever" to DeKalb. William Ezzard's Decatur Gold Mining Company was not the only one to incur substantial losses. The only known DeKalb citizen to make any money from the Dahlonega gold rush was Benjamin Franklin Swanton, who came to Decatur from Bath, Maine to sell mining equipment. The home he purchased from Ammi Williams in 1844 was said to be the nicest in Decatur. Swanton's descendants lived in the house on Atlanta Avenue until the mid-1960s, when they donated it to the DeKalb Historical Society. The house was moved to Decatur's Adair Park historic complex and restored, and is now maintained for the public to visit.

✧

The Baron DeKalb Chapter of the Daughters of the American Revolution erected this monument in 1945, marking the site of the first DeKalb Superior Court meeting at the home of William Jackson in the spring of 1823. The DeKalb Superior Court was part of several state circuits, but has been part of the Stone Mountain Circuit since 1855. Richard H. Clark was DeKalb's first judge of the Stone Mountain Circuit. Clark heard 28 criminal cases and 22 civil suits during his first term. The first criminal case involved James Hudgins, who was found guilty of simple larceny for stealing cows.

SPECIAL COLLECTIONS DEPARTMENT, GEORGIA STATE UNIVERSITY LIBRARY

The county's first real courthouse, "a neat brick building," was built in 1829 in the center of the Decatur Square by George Tomlinson at a cost of about $5,100.

In what is now the Brookhaven area of DeKalb, South Carolinians Solomon Goodwin and Samuel House settled about the same time near each other on Peachtree Road. Both the House and Goodwin houses are still standing about a mile apart. The Samuel House Federal-Style brick mansion, now the Peachtree Golf Club clubhouse, is DeKalb's finest example of classic antebellum architecture. The House mansion served as Sherman's headquarters during the Atlanta campaign in July 1864. However, the Goodwin house is a more realistic example of the kind of homes early DeKalb residents owned.

In December 1836, Governor William Schley signed legislation that would change the face of the county and the entire Southeast region. A new rail line was to terminate at "some point" on the southeastern bank of the Chattahoochee River. That "point" would become the city of Atlanta.

Prior to the decision, DeKalb residents vigorously debated where the terminus should be. Dr. Chapmon Powell favored Decatur. He was opposed by fellow state legislator James Calhoun as well as by a great many Decatur residents, who felt the railroad would be a detriment to their quiet community. Calhoun is said to have told Powell, "The terminus of that railroad will never be any more than an eating house." Powell responded, "True, and you will see the time when it will eat up Decatur."

When the railroad finally did come to Decatur, in 1845, the builders showed no regard for either opinion. They simply chose the most topographically suitable route.

Powell moved to Atlanta in 1850 and bought all the land where the Five Points area of downtown Atlanta is today. It is interesting to note that the land where Powell practiced medicine almost 200 years ago now contains the Veterans Administration Hospital, Emory University Hospital and Medical School, and the Centers for Disease Control and Prevention.

Decatur's townspeople were awakened on the night of January 9, 1842 when the "neat brick" courthouse burned. The cause remained a mystery, although many believed the fire was intentionally set or started by careless card players. All the county's records but the minutes of the Inferior Court were destroyed. A second brick courthouse was built on the same location.

Meanwhile, workers carved a rail line through the "wild unmolested forest" that was the western half of the county. Although there was not a cabin in sight, the place was called Terminus. A new town called Marthasville, named for Governor Wilson Lumpkin's daughter, quickly sprang up around the depot and was incorporated on December 23, 1843.

At first, "the rail road didn't start nowhere or go nowhere." The first locomotive, called *The Florida*, came to Marthasville aboard a wagon pulled by mules. The inaugural excursion took selected guests from Marthasville to Marietta, and people came from miles around to see the mechanical monster. It was said that there was not a person or dog left in Decatur.

Rebecca Latimer Felton, who experienced the first run, said that Marthasville at the time had one building, the depot, and an attached shed that doubled as a liquor store. Regular train service did not begin in Atlanta until three years later.

Chamber of commerce types believed that a small town with big city aspirations needed a name to match. J. Edgar Thomson is credited with the idea of calling the place Atlanta. The Georgia legislature approved of the new name and made it official in 1846.

Atlanta continued to grow rapidly, gaining new churches, a Masonic lodge, bank, two new newspapers, and several schools in 1847. The streets were "alive with people," many of them Northerners, bringing wares that previously required a trip to Augusta to acquire.

Decatur had its share of merchants, too, selling dry goods, groceries, medicines, saddles, hats, and general merchandise. A favorite entrepreneur was Aunt Seney Douglass, "a tall, fat old Negro woman of gingercake color, with a big soul, exuberant with cheerfulness, and a big chest," who sold ginger cakes and persimmon beer. During the 1840s, Decatur was not "wet," but a "little damp," especially during court weeks and on militia muster days and the Fourth of July. At other times temperance rallies provided a source of entertainment.

Atlanta held its first election on January 29, 1848. The new mayor, Moses W. Formwalt "was one of the boys." Drinking and gambling houses and cock fighting were the norm, and Saturday nights were a time for drunken brawls. Murrell's Row on Decatur Street and Snake Nation along Whitehall Road (later Peters Street) harbored criminals. DeKalb County indicted and convicted many criminals, but the county jail was too small and too distant from Atlanta to meet the need. In response to the number of crimes in Atlanta, DeKalb replaced its jail with a two-story building made of granite. Jonathan Norcross succeeded Formwalt as mayor, and vowed to reclaim the town.

As Decatur approached the new decade of 1850, it was said to be "a pretty village... proverbially healthy," while Atlanta was "an overgrown town with none of the marks of a city." Atlanta had more than four times the residents of Decatur.

Although considerable business had moved away from Decatur to Atlanta, the coming of the railroad enabled the growth of the granite industry around Stone Mountain. John T.

Glenn, S. M. Inman, and J. A. Alexander chartered the county's first successful quarry, the Stone Mountain Granite and Railway Company, in 1869. Milling was the primary industry in DeKalb—grist mills for grinding grain and saw mills for creating lumber. Every stream large enough to generate water power sufficient to turn a mill wheel accommodated a small mill. Many a farmer subsidized his farm income by turning his neighbor's grain into flour and trees into lumber.

DeKalb County's second city cemetery originated on June 6, 1850, when the county purchased six acres of land southeast of the town limits of Atlanta. First called Atlanta Cemetery, the name was later changed to Oakland. There was much need for a cemetery in a town where the criminal element ruled. Ruffians tried to persuade Mayor Jonathan Norcross to resign by blasting his store with sand and gravel fired from the 1812 cannon, which they stole from the Decatur courthouse grounds. Norcross retaliated with a midnight raid on the Rowdy Party headquarters. The Rowdies were run out of town, and their hideouts torched.

DeKalb County would no longer have to worry about trying to control crime in Atlanta after December 20, 1853, the day Fulton County was created, with Atlanta the county seat. Shortly after Atlanta's incorporation, the DeKalb Grand Jury reported an "almost entire absence of criminal business."

The Georgia General Assembly incorporated the Reverend John S. Wilson's Hannah Moore Female Collegiate Institute. It would be another thirty-five years before boys had a similar institution, the Donald Fraser High School. While Decatur schools were thought to provide the best education, there were small schools throughout the county. Fraser closed shortly after the city of Decatur organized its public school system in 1901.

DeKalb County approached the new decade in 1860 with a population just shy of six thousand. By comparison, Fulton County was almost double the residents. DeKalb's population included almost fifteen hundred slaves, considerably fewer than Georgia counties with a plantation economy.

DeKalb had always been a Union county, and on January 2, 1861, elected two Union delegates—Charles Murphey of Decatur and George K. Smith of Stone Mountain—to the Georgia Secession Convention. Murphey prayed he died before he saw the state secede. His prayer was answered, as he died on opening day of the convention.

Charles Murphey's only daughter, Eliza, had married Milton Anthony Candler, who was a state senator and representative and a U.S. representative during the difficult days of Reconstruction. Descendants of this family are still active in DeKalb today.

Edward L. Morton raised the first homemade Confederate flag in DeKalb, atop a poplar tree near Williams' Mill on Peachtree Creek a few miles from Decatur. A sign of the county's divided sentiment, the Morton family cared for a Union soldier during the occupation of Decatur. Local lore says that the Confederate flag flew from the tree until Sherman's soldiers cut it down. Thirteen sprouts are said to have grown from the stump.

While most able-bodied men marched off to war, Decatur's women set up shop at the home of Ezekiel Mason to sew uniforms and banners. Mary Gay knitted socks and sent them, along with personal letters and poems, to commanding officers who distributed them to grateful soldiers. Gay was one of the few Decatur residents who refused to flee the city during the occupation by Sherman's soldiers. Her heroic actions enabling her neighbors to survive the invasion are recounted in her book, *Life in Dixie During the War*.

Pressure mounted on men who had not already enlisted, but many in DeKalb were Union supporters. Especially in the Tucker area, men hid in secluded camps. Two men, John and Joel Morris, were said to have been killed for their pro-Union views.

Decatur High School's band and majorettes are pictured with the school in the background in August of 1950. The city of Decatur's school system began operation in 1902 and currently has one high school, one middle school, and four elementary schools.

SPECIAL COLLECTIONS DEPARTMENT, GEORGIA STATE UNIVERSITY LIBRARY

Above: Citizens gathered in the heart of East Atlanta, at the intersection of Flat Shoals and Glenwood Avenues, on December 15, 1937, to unveil a marker commemorating the Civil War Battle of Atlanta. Governor E. D. Rivers, Atlanta Mayor William B. Hartsfield, and DeKalb County Commissioner Charles A. Matthews were on hand for the ceremonies. Atlanta artist and historian Wilbur G. Kurtz gave an address. The marker was presented by E. A. Minor of the of the Minor Lodge No. 603 F. & A.M. J. S. McWilliams and Jean Peeple, son and great granddaughter of John W. McWilliams, a solder in the Battle of Atlanta, unveiled the marker.

COURTESY OF THE THE EVERITT FAMILY

Below: The city of Doraville celebrated its centennial in 1971. As part of the shenanigans, members of the north DeKalb law firm, Gerstein and Carter, participate in a skit in which a sheriff gets the drop on some evildoers. "Sheriff" Richard F. (Dick) Livingston is pictured with "moonshiners" Joe W. Gerstein, Edward E. Carter, and J. David Chesnut (standing, left to right), and Hugh R. (Rick) Powell, kneeling. Chesnut, whose family has lived in DeKalb for several generations, was chairman of the MARTA board from 1987 to 1988.

SPECIAL COLLECTIONS DEPARTMENT, GEORGIA STATE UNIVERSITY LIBRARY

The year 1864 was the harshest in the county's history. It began with daytime temperatures of eight degrees in January. Confederate money was worthless, and food was scarce. Letters from soldiers brought horrific descriptions of fighting and death.

When Union soldiers captured the town of Roswell on July 6, 1864, DeKalb residents began to bury their valuables and pack up necessities in preparation to leave the war zone. The invading army crossed the Chattahoochee River into Fulton and north DeKalb on July 9. From there Union troops marched to Stone Mountain and Decatur.

On July 22, when Wheeler's cavalry drove the federal troops through the city to the north, Mary Gay's house was between the Confederate and Union battle lines. "Shot and shell flew in all direction, and the shingles on the roof were following suit, and the leaves and the limbs and the bark of the trees were descending in showers so heavy as almost to obscure the view of the contending forces." A victory by the Confederates was short-lived, and Decatur surrendered to the Union army.

Major General James B. McPherson's troops were strung out on both sides of the railroad between Decatur and Atlanta. As Wheeler and Schofield dueled in Decatur, McPherson's soldiers fought for the main prize, the city of Atlanta. McPherson was killed by Confederate troops on what is now Monument Avenue, just south of I-20, in East Atlanta. After the war, East Atlanta patriarch James (Spanish Jim) Brown deeded land for a McPherson monument to the U.S. Army.

Fighting in and around Atlanta lasted from until August 9, and the burning of the city commenced. Confederate troops pulled out of Atlanta on August 31, and Atlanta surrendered on September 2. The Union army slowly moved out of Decatur and headed through southeast DeKalb and beyond, burning many homes as they went and leaving behind destitute people. Devastation was so complete that citizens claimed that no bluebirds were seen in Decatur for three years.

As soon as the soldiers were gone, the refugees began returning to Decatur. One of the first tasks was rebuilding Decatur Presbyterian Church, which never suspended church or Sunday school meetings, even when the building was occupied by the Union army. Church services were held in homes, sometimes attended only by women and old men.

DeKalb's final war-related death was an innocent civilian. Sarah (Sallie) Durham, 17, and her family had just returned to their Sycamore Street home after waiting out the war at her grandmother's home. On September 1, 1865, while standing at a window watching a train pass, Sallie was hit by a bullet recklessly fired by a Union soldier.

A year after the surrender, on April 26, 1866, DeKalb celebrated the first Confederate Memorial Day. Women formed the Atlanta Ladies Memorial Association and began the grim task of removing bodies of Confederate dead from the places where they had lain for more than a year. These dedicated women arranged for proper burials for all.

In response to the war's saddest consequence, Dr. Jesse Boring of south DeKalb opened The Orphan's Home of the North Georgia Conference of the Methodist Church in Norcross in 1871. The orphanage burned two years later, and the church moved the home to Columbia Drive in Decatur, where it is still located today.

The new Atlanta and Charlotte Air Line Railroad (later Southern Railway) began its march from Atlanta through north DeKalb, resulting in towns like Doraville (1871) and Chamblee (1908). Town lore says that incorporation of Doraville was precipitated by the desire of residents to control saloons that sprang up near the railroad depot.

Publishers of a new Atlanta weekly literary magazine called *Sunny South* turned to Clarkston when looking for an editor. Poet and novelist Mary Edwards Bryan edited the publication for ten years beginning in 1874 and wrote fifteen books, becoming one of the highest-paid women of her time. A memorial on the grounds of the Clarkston Women's Club describes her as a "beloved daughter of Clarkston and one of Georgia's most famous women."

Bryan once wrote that Clarkston had "magnificent trees, pure air, excellent water, an unequaled train service, good schools and churches, well equipped stores, a handsome Masonic lodge, many beautiful and some elegant homes, and a grand university [Lamar University] in process of erection. The town is notable for its morality, its utter freedom from all objectionable characters—white or black... There is no calaboose in Clarkston; none is needed." A new post office opened in the community of Clarkston on October 9, 1876; the town would not be incorporated for another six years.

One of DeKalb's most famous mills, operated by Washington J. Houston, opened in 1876 on the South Fork of Peachtree Creek between Clifton and LaVista roads. Houston Mill, on property Houston purchased from his father-in-law Dr. Chapmon Powell, produced cornmeal until 1940. Houston built the county's first hydroelectric plant on the site about 1900 and flipped the switch on the county's first electric light in his home that same year. Three years later Houston's company, Decatur Light, Power and Water, would supply electricity to the town of Decatur.

The first light bulb was followed by the first telephone, installed in Decatur in 1884. A five-minute call to Atlanta, considered long distance, cost fifteen cents.

The year 1881 saw the completion of a privately-owned railroad in north DeKalb after more than twenty years of on-and-off construction. The railroad ran from the south bank of the Chattahoochee River to the Atlanta and Charlotte Air-Line Railroad in Roswell Junction (later Chamblee). Stops along the way were in Dunwoody, Wilson's Mill (Peeler and North Shallowford roads) and Morgan Falls (now in Fulton County). Isaac Martin (Ike) Roberts was the only engineer in the Roswell Railroad's 40-year history. The small-gauge railroad took products like

✧

Left: Mayor Ed Sutton is pictured on the steps of Clarkston's first city hall in about 1930. The city was chartered in 1882 and named for Col. W. W. Clark, a director of the Georgia Railroad, along which the town was built. First called New Siding for section foreman Jake New, Clarkston acquired the nickname of Goatsville, due to the inordinate number of goats owned by the townspeople. The Clarkston High School mascot is the Angora goat. Clarkston is home to the third oldest women's club building in the United States.

Below: William Mitchell Morrison, left, was a DeKalb state representative and senator, as well as a judge. He led the campaign to defeat a turn-of-the-century attempt to move the county seat from Decatur to Stone Mountain. His father, J. J. Morrison, right, is said to have given Jefferson Davis $20,000 in gold to launch the first Confederate cavalry unit. This photo, featuring the toddler, Maria Fleeta Hewitt, was used on top of a cigar box for the EEM Tobacco (later Reynolds) Company. The company was named for Edward Edmonia Morrison, daughter of J. J. Morrison.

✧

Top, left: Willie Vilenah (Miss Willie) Medlock and Daniel Johnson are pictured on their wedding day, March 22, 1887. Named for both her parents (William Parks Medlock and Virginia Vilenah Antoinette Mason), she is the only woman in DeKalb history to have two streets named after her—Willivee Drive and Vilenah Lane. Willivee runs between North Decatur and North Druid Hills roads. Vilenah Lane is in the Druid Hills neighborhood, off Oakdale Road. Medlock Road and the Medlock community were named for her family.

Top, right: Built in 1891, Agnes Scott Hall, left, was the first building on the Agnes Scott College campus in Decatur. With its distinctive bell tower, the building is still an integral part of the campus. Founded in 1889 as Decatur Female Seminary, the school was renamed in 1890 for Agnes Irvine Scott, mother of the school's chief benefactor, George Washington Scott. The Reverend Frank Henry Gaines, minister of Decatur Presbyterian Church, was the school's first president.

Right: Hooper Alexander was Charles Murphey Candler's law partner and served in the state legislature at the same time. He also was one of the incorporators of the original Stone Mountain Confederate Monumental Association. However, he is best known for seeking the commutation of the death sentence of Leo Frank in 1913, a move which may have cost him his political career. One of the documents on his desk is an advertisement for dry cleaning suits at a cost of fifty cents each.

lumber and vegetables to market and returned with manufactured goods from Sears Roebuck and other mail order houses. "Old Buck" enabled a much-heralded visit to DeKalb of President Theodore Roosevelt in 1905.

DeKalb got a new tax receiver in 1883. H. H. Burgess was the first in a long line of office holders and public servants. Ben B. Burgess was clerk of the DeKalb Superior Court in the mid twentieth century, serving the longest stint of the total of eighty-seven years a Burgess held this office. Robert Burgess served as chief of police.

Two years later, two controversies kept people talking. Since the western half of DeKalb was made into Fulton in 1853, some residents believed that Decatur was no longer centrally located enough to be convenient to all citizens. They wanted the county seat

Left: J. W. McWilliams, second from right, opened his store at Glenwood and Flat Shoals in East Atlanta on Thanksgiving Day, 1889. In addition to general merchandise, he sold notions, hardware, groceries, and stock feed. The store also became East Atlanta's first post office in 1891. McWilliams, who died in 1934 at age ninety, was the first postmaster.
COURTESY OF THE EVERITT FAMILY.

Bottom, left: This tiny structure once served as the courthouse where justices of the peace conducted business for Militia District 572. Originally located in the heart of Tucker at LaVista and Fellowship, the Brownings Courthouse was cited in reports of federal military operations in July of 1864. The structure was moved to the grounds of the Tucker Recreation Center on LaVista Road in the mid-1980s. Pictured in 1983 are DeKalb Historical Society president Peggy Hill and Tucker attorney and historian Charles Alford.

Bottom, right: The Stone Mountain memorial carving was completed in 1970, and for the second time dignitaries celebrated with lunch on General Lee's shoulder. From left are Mary Payne, Tom Elliott, William Kenny, Roy Faulkner, Ben Fortson, Tommy Irvin, Lane Mitchell, and Arthur Bolton.

moved to Stone Mountain. The issue was resolved in 1897, with the county seat remaining in Decatur.

Twenty years after the end of the Civil War, German artists came to DeKalb to research the site of the Battle of Atlanta in preparation to create a unique commemorative painting. The result was a cyclorama, a circular panoramic picture, the largest painting in the country. After touring, the painting was first exhibited in Atlanta in the 1890s. It is currently housed at Atlanta's Grant Park.

DeKalb got its first Commissioners of Roads and Revenues in 1887, thanks to state legislation written by Charles Murphey Candler. Candler's son Scott Candler would become DeKalb's most famous commissioner. The original board members were T. U. Hightower, Thomas J. Flake, E. J. Bond, L. N. Nash, and William C. Holbrook. The commissioners had their work cut out for them just repairing the county's miserable roads. One near Snapfinger Creek had a hole sufficient to overturn a buggy and cause the drowning of a horse.

In a downtown Atlanta pharmacy, John Pemberton invented a headache remedy in

✧

Above: DeKalb's third courthouse was brand new when this photo was taken in 1898. Made of local granite, the exterior survived when the courthouse burned in 1916, but the cupola was destroyed. When the courthouse was rebuilt, a new cupola was not installed, but a clock was placed in the gable. East and west wings were added later.

1886. DeKalb resident Asa Candler took an interest, and by 1891 owned the formula for Coca-Cola. The headache remedy soon became a "delicious, refreshing, exhilarating, invigorating" soft drink. Candler's financial success would benefit DeKalb County in many ways.

The biggest attraction in DeKalb in the 1880s, especially for children, was the annual county Sunday School Celebration held at The Tabernacle, an open-sided shelter at the corner of College Avenue and Commerce Drive. Decatur was filled with the sounds of three thousand attendees coming together and children loudly singing such favorites as Bringing in the Sheaves. Midday was quiet, while families enjoyed home-cooked chicken and pound cake.

A newcomer to Decatur—Dr. Frank Henry Gaines—became the pastor of Decatur Presbyterian Church in the late 1880s. He had a philosophy that struck a chord with George Washington Scott, who was described as one of the most generous and public-spirited citizens ever to reside in Decatur. Gaines believed that "if you educate a man, you may produce a good citizen, but if you educate a woman, you may train a whole family." With Scott as the major benefactor, Gaines opened the Decatur Female Seminary in 1889. The school's name was changed to Agnes Scott Institute in honor of Scott's mother. The school became a four-year, degree-granting college in 1906.

Two new cities—Kirkwood and Edgewood—were incorporated in the early 1890s in an effort to control the crime that spilled out of Atlanta and unincorporated areas. Both were absorbed into Atlanta. Although DeKalb had fewer than 20,000 residents in 1890, newcomers flocked to the fresh air, pure water, and elbow room of the suburbs, none of which could be found in Atlanta.

Decatur Presbyterian Church was forced to build a new sanctuary in 1891, due to the number of Agnes Scott College students who attended services there. The $18,000 facility would last the church another sixty years.

The town of Panola on the South River, the oldest industrial site in the Atlanta area, disappeared during the last decade of the nineteenth century. Robert Clarke's Panola Cotton Mill burned, and the Oglethorpe textile mill closed. The Panola Power Company was built on the site.

The towns of Tucker and nearby Montreal came into being in the 1890s, but only Tucker would survive. One disaster after another doomed Montreal. The town was planned with the Montreal Manufacturing Company in its center, bringing jobs making a variety of products from furniture to toys. Financial difficulties forced the partially-constructed factory to be sold for a mere $250. Attempted re-use of the factory's boiler resulted in a deadly explosion, and subsequent attempts to revive the town also failed.

Dr. Washington Jackson Houston, Jr. became DeKalb's first county physician (the beginning of the county's public health department) near the turn of the century. The son-in-law of DeKalb's first doctor, Chapmon Powell, he moved his office from the Powell home place to the Square in Decatur. The house, which is still standing, was rotated so that it faced Church Street instead of the Square.

Atlantans looking to move to a splendid new upscale subdivision in 1893 would have to wait. The financial crisis of 1893 forced Joel Hurt to

scrap plans for his neighborhood designed by famed Central Park designer Fredrick Law Olmsted. The property was sold in 1908 to a syndicate headed by Asa G. Candler.

DeKalb began work in 1898 on a new granite courthouse, equipped with a special room for ladies, complete with toilets. Walls were constructed of two layers of bricks made in Decatur and covered with granite from Lithonia. The cost was $60,000.

At the close of the nineteenth century, DeKalb County was still a primarily rural county, as it would remain for the next fifty years. With fewer than 10,000 residents, there were only 2,750 students in 55 white public schools and 1,500 students in the county's 17 black public schools.

However, Decatur already displayed many of the attributes that would make DeKalb Atlanta's bedroom community of the future, one of which was a new electric train line between the two cities. "As a suburban place of residence for Atlanta it just simply has no equal, and with its three different lines of transportation that link it so closely to the city, it is now just as convenient for Atlanta people to live at as Inman Park, West End or any of the immediate suburbs adjoining the city limits," reported *The Atlanta Constitution*. A train ride from Atlanta to Decatur cost a nickel.

Granite mining proved profitable in the last half of the nineteenth century, but it soared after 1900, when an industrious Scotsman launched what became a huge granite empire. John Keay (Jack) Davidson came from Aberdeen, Scotland to Lithonia in 1887 at the age of 17 and first worked for Southern Granite at "Big Ledge." He and John Daugherty defied the striking Paving Block Cutters Union in 1900 and rented the quarry. Six years later, Davidson successfully outbid competitor Samuel Venable for purchase. Big Ledge and other southeast DeKalb quarries produced millions of huge paving blocks and aggregate, curbing, and building stones the size of sofas that were shipped to the nation's largest cities and around the world.

Of 17 granite companies operating in Stone Mountain and Lithonia during the Depression, only Davidson remained open, thanks not to large pieces of granite, but to the tiniest pebbles. Jack Davidson let his sons, Charlie, Norton, Keay, and Wheeler handle the business of crushing waste stone into a product that facilitates digestion in chickens. From a small experiment, the Stone Mountain Grit Company became the world's largest suppliers of chicken grit, which they called Stonemo.

The company continued producing Stonemo after the Depression and resumed quarrying building stone at four plants, including Arabia Mountain. Meanwhile, the Davidsons became active members of the Lithonia community, with "Mr. Charlie" serving as mayor (1946-1955) and chairman of the DeKalb Board of Education (1950-1962). At one point, Lithonia had a population of 1,250 residents, and 50 of them were Davidsons. Charles Davidson Jr. succeeded his father as company president. Today a portion of the Davidson property is the Davidson-Arabia Mountain Nature Preserve, part of the federal 2,450-acre Arabia Mountain Heritage Area, which includes the Lyon House, the county's oldest home, and the Vaughters farm, the last working farm in the county.

The 1900s saw the demise of the county's Confederate veterans, including three Wallace brothers.

✧

When George Washington Scott opened Scottdale Mills in 1901, it was the centerpiece of a traditional Southern mill town. For many years the cotton mill was one of only two industries in the county, the other being granite mining. While the mill closed in 1982, the homes are still there, many of them occupied by retired mill workers or their descendants. The mill was only one of the many business interests of Scott, who died in 1903. The Scott family ran Georgia Duck and Cordage in Avondale from 1918 until a British company bought it in 1998. Plans unveiled in 2006 to redevelop the property as an expansion of Avondale's Tudor village have yet to materialize. Scottdale is best known today as home of the DeKalb Farmer's Market, which began in 1977 as a produce stand.

William R. Wallace was famous for the furniture built at his mill on Nancy Creek at Chamblee Dunwoody Road. Dr. Luther C. Fischer, co-founder of Crawford Long Hospital bought the site from the Wallace estate in 1909. Architect Phillip Trammel Schutze designed the brick home that sat on a dramatic prominence overlooking the creek in 1930. The grounds of Flowerland featured a garden so spectacular that people came from miles around, especially in spring when the roses and azaleas were in bloom. The home since has been used as a girls' school and a church and is now being renovated as part of a residential complex.

William's brother, John, operated a furniture shop, sawmill, and business village where Peavine Creek merged with the South Fork of Peachtree Creek. The village on the Seaboard Railroad, about a mile northwest of the spot where Emory University is today, once had a post office and a railroad flag station, both called "Wallace." John Wallace closed his mill in 1900, and the village had disappeared by 1917 or 1918. The third brother, Thomas Wallace, produced his potable, "Stone Mountain Corn," until 1920.

Agnes Scott College benefactor George Washington Scott opened Scottdale Mill in 1901 followed by the Georgia Duck and Cordage Mill in Avondale. The Scottdale mill was the centerpiece of a traditional mill village. Although the mill closed in 1982, several of the mill houses are still standing. Georgia Duck and Cordage was acquired by a British firm in 1998.

Conrad L. Allgood was the Scottdale Mill staff physician, and traveled the county treating other patients in Scottdale, Clarkston, Decatur, and Avondale. Dr. Allgood bought his first Ford in 1914 for $290. He wore out numerous horses and buggies, as well as 27 Fords, during his 40 years in medicine.

In 1904 the Atlanta Athletic Club purchased the East Lake amusement park as a site for two new golf courses. Atlanta newspapers praised the new club and courses, even calling the new access road a "speedway… built especially for automobilists." The town of East Lake was incorporated in 1908 but became part of the city of Atlanta in 1924. The town became the new home of Bobby Jones, and the courses the launching pad for his extraordinary career.

After the club moved in 1966, the East Lake Meadows public housing complex was built on one course, while the other remained a golfing venue. During the next twenty years

This distinctive three-gabled house was the homeplace of John Wilson McCurdy and his wife, Sarah Ann (Sallie) Carter. They lived at 5406 Mountain Street in Stone Mountain for many years. Although the house has been torn down, their stone hitching post is still in its original location. Pictured, left to right, are John Steve McCurdy, Robert Fletcher Wells, William Tarlton McCurdy, Ida McCurdy Wells, Carl Thomas Wells, Sallie McCurdy Haynie, John Dean Wells, John Wilson McCurdy, Sallie Carter McCurdy, William S. McCurdy, Myrtice McCurdy, and a Mr. Wood. Carl Thomas Wells cut the stone for the 1898 county courthouse, today's home of the DeKalb History Center.

COURTESY OF DOTTIE SPENCER.

the East Lake community deteriorated to the point that the crime rate soared to18 times the national average, employment sank to 13.5 percent, and fewer than a third of students graduated high school. Local police called East Lake Meadows a "war zone."

In an effort spearheaded by real estate developer Tom Cousins, the East Lake Foundation, formed in 1995, restored the golf club, which has served as a catalyst for a remarkable neighborhood renewal. The housing project was replaced with a mixed-income apartment complex. The community now has a new charter school, a YMCA, and a public golf course, which is home to The First Tee, a golf and mentoring program for area youths. In 2006 crime was down 95 percent, and all students were expected to graduate. One golf tournament each year benefits community programs. The East Lake golf course is rated one of the top 100 in the world.

William Schley Howard, DeKalb's "picturesque" defense attorney, elected to the U.S. House of Representatives in 1910, beginning an eighty-year legacy of elected service among Howard family members. Howard, the son of Thomas Coke Howard, Atlanta's Civil War postmaster, was famous for his work in more than five hundred murder cases. His grandson, Pierre Howard Jr., served as a state senator and two terms as lieutenant governor, from 1991-1999.

Flivver fever hit DeKalb around 1910, and soon there were an unprecedented three car dealerships on the Square in Decatur. But, there was only one paved road in the county—from Decatur to Stone Mountain along the Georgia Railroad—and drivers and passengers often had to get out and push their cars.

The early 1900s brought to DeKalb a popular couple who would make their individual marks on Decatur and the county. Guy Hudson, youngest son of Thomas Pliney Hudson, and his bride, the former Mary Jackson Haralson, moved to the elder Hudson's farm on Clairmont Road after their marriage in 1911. They later moved to Oakland Street. Guy Hudson became head of the city water department and operated a grocery and notions store on the corner of Sycamore and McDonough. When he died in 1937, his wife took a job with the newly-organized DeKalb Chamber of Commerce. She stayed with the Chamber until 1957, moving up from secretary to executive director and executive vice president. Although she received national recognition as one of the few women in this field, she

✧

A large crowd gathered at the courthouse on April 25, 1908 for the dedication of the Confederate monument. The monument is inscribed on four sides in part: "How well they kept the faith is faintly written in the records of the armies and the history of the times. We who knew them testify that as their courage was without a precedent their fortitude has been without a parallel, may their posterity be worthy. Erected by the men, women and children of DeKalb County to the memory of the soldiers and sailors of the Confederacy of whose virtues in peace and in war we are witnesses to the end that justice may be done and that the truth perish not."

✧

Right: Scott Candler, (front row, left) organized Decatur Boy Scout Troop No. 1 some time before this trip to Cleveland, Georgia. in the summer of 1913. The troop was the first Boy Scout troop organized in the South.

Below: The Hopkins-Haygood Gate, dedicated in 1937 to two nineteenth-century Emory presidents, marks the university's main entrance on North Decatur Road. The pillar at left is dedicated to Atticus Greene Haygood, who graduated from Emory College in 1859, fifty-six years before the University moved from Oxford to Atlanta. The pillar at right is dedicated to Isaac Stiles Hopkins, also an 1859 graduate of Emory College. Hopkins went on to be the founder and first president of the Georgia School of Technology (forerunner of the Georgia Institute of Technology). The gateway was a gift of Linton B. Robeson, a member of the Class of 1886. Hopkins and Haygood are credited with keeping the school alive during Reconstruction.

COURTESY OF THE MANUSCRIPT, ARCHIVES, AND RARE BOOK LIBRARY, EMORY UNIVERSITY.

described herself as "just a grandmother making a living." Hudson was fondly known as "DeKalb's Grandma" until her death in 1970.

Two Candler brothers—Asa and Warren—were instrumental in bringing to DeKalb the county's largest university. The university opened in 1915 on Druid Hills property donated by Asa who provided a large endowment. Warren was the first chancellor. One of Emory's most unusual graduates was Eleanore Raoul, who went on to found the Atlanta Equal Suffrage Party and led an Equal Rights Amendment parade in 1974 at the age of eighty-five.

Emory is the centerpiece of the "Clifton Corridor," a mile-long stretch of Clifton Road that also contains the U.S. Centers for Disease Control and Prevention, the Yerkes Primate Center, and the American Cancer Society headquarters.

After folding 40 years earlier, Oglethorpe University made Brookhaven its new home in 1915. The school's dynamic president, Dr. Thornwell Jacobs, created worldwide controversy over his search for the grave of Georgia's founder, James Edward Oglethorpe. The university's Crypt of Civilization time capsule, sealed in 1940, is scheduled to be re-opened in the year 8113.

Scottish Rite Convalescent Home for Crippled Children opened in 1915 in two small, wood-framed cottages in Decatur as a facility where indigent, crippled children who had surgery at other hospitals could recuperate. A new fifty-bed Scottish Rite Hospital for Crippled Children opened in 1919. The hospital moved to north Atlanta in the 1970s.

Firefighters were called again to downtown Decatur on a morning in September of 1916 to save the county courthouse. A photograph in the *Atlanta Constitution* shows the time at 5:20 a.m.; five minutes later the grand cupola and "Justice" statue collapsed. Only the exterior of the building burned; the thick Lithonia granite walls survived to provide the foundation for

Left The Scottish Rite Crippled Children's Home building in the Oakhurst community of Decatur was built around 1919. Today the building has new life as The Solarium at Old Scottish Rite. The Community Center of South Decatur was founded in 1979 with the mission of offering "programs and services for the assistance, education, and enjoyment of the Decatur community, "as well as to preserve and maintain the historic buildings. The Solarium is available for rental, and is a venue for community meetings and classes, as well as entertainment events, such as the BBQ, Blues and Bluegrass Festival.

COURTESY OF THE JOE LEE' COLLECTION.

the Old Courthouse that is home to the DeKalb History Center today. Fireproof safes protected most of the county's records. The cause was thought to be a smoldering cigar butt dropped by someone in the crowd waiting for election results the night before.

Care of military veterans in the Atlanta area began in 1919 when the federal government purchased the Cheston W. King Hospital on Peachtree Road near Oglethorpe University. The facility later became known as the "Old 48," the numerical designation given by the federal government. When old Camp Gordon reopened as the Naval Air Station during World War II, the Lawson Veterans Hospital was built as an amputation and neurological center for allied wounded and for German and Italian prisoners of war. Both hospitals were replaced by the Veterans Administration Hospital on Clairmont Road, which opened in 1966.

The 1920s began with another burst of generosity by Asa Candler, who donated $1.25 million to move Wesley Memorial Hospital to the campus of Emory University.

Below: Fresh from a horse show, mounted Shriners gathered on the grounds of the Scottish Rite Convalescent Home for Crippled Children in Decatur in 1946. The brainchild of Mrs. Bertie Wardlow and Dr. Michael Hoke, the facility began in 1915 as two cottages for children to recuperate after surgery at other hospitals. A fifty-bed orthopedic hospital designed by Neel Reid opened in 1919, with salaries and supplies paid for by the Scottish Rite Masons. The hospital moved to north Atlanta in the 1970s and merged with Decatur's Egleston Children's Hospital to form Children's Healthcare of Atlanta in 1998.

COURTESY OF THE SPECIAL COLLECTIONS DEPARTMENT, GEORGIA STATE UNIVERSITY LIBRARY

✧

Right: Avondale Estates founder George Willis wanted "every known help to healthful play" for the town's children. To that end he built 30 acres of parks, playgrounds, and athletic fields into his subdivision. This bench and pergola was located in the plaza area.

COURTESY OF T. MARTIN-HART, FORKNER COLLECTION.

Below: By 1926 the first houses in Avondale Estates had been built along Clarendon Avenue, one of the few paved streets in DeKalb. According to George Willis' vision, the town would be planted with 14 miles of pink crepe myrtles, dogwood and redbud trees, as well as 253 abelia bushes which still screen homes from the business district. The "only documented example of a planned new town in the Southeast," Avondale Estates was placed on the National Register of Historic Places in 1986.

COURTESY OF T. MARTIN-HART, FORKNER COLLECTION.

Candler had launched the hospital by purchasing the Calico House, the colorful home of the Marcus Bell family in downtown Atlanta in 1904. The facility changed its name to Emory University Hospital in 1925. Warren Candler was the first president of the hospital's board of trustees.

In the 1920s, another university—Columbia Theological Seminary—moved to Decatur from Columbia, South Carolina.

A small, rural post office opened on February 20, 1892, in the community of Ingleside, but the post office, the community, and the name of Ingleside would become a distant memory after 1924. Entrepreneur and "promoter extraordinaire" George Francis Willis bought the village, as well as several large farms, and transformed it into the Southeast's first planned community. Patterned after the English birthplace of William Shakespeare, the town was called Avondale Estates and the downtown buildings designed in Tudor style. In addition to stately homes, Avondale Estates was designed with a lake, tennis courts, clubhouse, riding stable, vegetable garden, plant nursery, dairy, playgrounds, and a swimming pool for residents. The town was planted with 14 miles of crape myrtles, dogwood, redbud, and red maple trees and a long hedge of abelia to screen residences from the commercial area.

Willis gathered a significant team of architects, engineers, planners, and managers to make the project work. Among those was Ben Sands Forkner, who was general manager and superintendent. Bessie and Ben Forkner and their seven children became valuable citizens, with Ben being involved in education,

agriculture, commerce, banking, and real estate. Several of his children also worked in the family real estate business, and son Tom was one of the founders of the Waffle House chain, which originated in Avondale.

Leila Ross Wilburn was among the architects who designed houses in Avondale Estates, as well as Decatur, Druid Hills, Ansley Park, Candler Park, and Midtown Atlanta. The Decatur resident was one of only two female architects in Georgia when she accepted her first commission in 1907 at the age of 22. She is noted for her innovative pattern book from which clients could choose house patterns.

Avondale Estates was incorporated in 1925. Willis died in 1932, but development of Avondale Estates continued into the 1950s. The population, originally planned to be 2,000 residents, had grown to 2,609 in 2000. The Avondale Estates Historic District was listed in the National Register of Historic Places in 1986.

The train pulled out of the Decatur station in early 1927, bound for Washington, D.C. On board were Leslie Jasper Steele, recently elected as the new DeKalb representative to the U.S. House, and his family. Steele, with his wife and eight children, were said to be the largest congressional family in Washington. In addition to being a teacher and lawyer, Steele's list of public service included being county school commissioner, secretary and treasurer of the first Decatur School Board, Decatur mayor, city and county attorney, and state representative. He served in the U.S. House until 1929, when he died in office.

The DeKalb Barons baseball team gave residents some relief from the worries of the Depression, when in 1930 they met the Macon Peaches for the title of best sandlot

✧

Top, left: George F. Willis gave a barbecue in 1926 to officially open Avondale Estates and to acknowledge his supporters and those who helped make his dream city a reality. Willis, the founder of Avondale Estates and one-time chairman of the Stone Mountain Confederate Monumental Association, made his fortune in proprietary medicine. He died on July 20, 1934, at the age of 53 and was buried in Waynesville, N. C.

COURTESY OF T. MARTIN-HART, FORKNER COLLECTION.

Top, right: Ingleside was a pleasant village near Covington Highway until the mid 1920s, when George Francis Willis chose it to be the site of a new planned community. A trip to England's Stratford-On-Avon inspired the Tudor style buildings and the name Avondale Estates. Avondale Estates became a city in 1928 after its residents adopted the first city charter.

COURTESY OF T. MARTIN-HART, FORKNER COLLECTION.

Bottom: The first Waffle House (Unit 1) restaurant opened on Labor Day in 1955 on College Avenue in Avondale Estates, although the first photo of the restaurant was not taken until the mid-1960s. Founded by Joe Rogers and Tom Forkner, the chain now has more than 1,500 restaurants in 25 states. The company has restored Unit 1 and opened the third of September as a Waffle House museum. A competitor, Huddle House, started in Decatur in 1964. Huddle House statistics answer the age-old question: hash browns or grits? At Huddle House, hash browns are holding a slight lead.

Right: Baseball fever hit DeKalb during the 1930s. The county had six teams: the DeKalb Barons and teams from Scottdale Mills, Lithonia, Belmont, Chamblee, Flat Rock, and Decatur. They all were involved in intense rivalries, but pulled together when the Barons met the Macon team for state bragging rights. Members of the Barons team from an unknown year are (front row, left to right) Julian Mason, Julian Chase, and Hugh Trotti. In the second row are Robert Barry, Curtis Thompson, Thompson [first name unknown], Tom Alston, Eugene Hardeman, and Erskine Reese. In the back row are Wallace Daily, Bayne Gipson, and John Reese.

Below: DeKalb County had only two library branches—Decatur and Lithonia—in the 1930s, when Maud Burrus' personal car became the first bookmobile. The county obtained its first real bookmobile through the federal Works Progress Administration in the late 1930s. Louise Trotti drove the bookmobile, taking reading materials to homes, service station, schools, post offices—anywhere people might be in need of books.

team in Georgia. The Barons staged a "smashing comeback" to win 15-13 after two outs in the ninth inning. DeKalb baseball fans benefited from great sandlot rivalries among teams from Scottdale Mill, Lithonia, Belmont, Chamblee, and Decatur.

A radical concept—parking places for automobiles—came to Emory Village in 1937. The popularity of shopping centers continued through the decades, with strip centers popping up through the 1950s and '60s. North DeKalb Mall opened in 1965 as an open-air mall, but was enclosed soon after. It was the first air-conditioned mall in the area.

Although DeKalb already had two libraries—Lithonia and Decatur—libraries really began to blossom in the 1940s with the influx of families into the county. Louise Trotti and Barbara Loar are the architects of the DeKalb Library System. Trotti, who served for 38 years, 20 as director, began her career driving the bookmobile. During her tenure, the county gained seven library branches and books were made available to inmates. Loar was director from 1982 to 1991, during which time branches more than doubled and books increased by sixty percent.

Left: The Decatur Rotary Club held its first meeting in April 1938. Members present were (standing, left to right) Dr. Robert B. Holt, Dr. D. W. Leary, P. H. Carmichael, S. N. Forrester Jr., Max S. Weil, Dr. Carl Pickett, Dean C. J. Hilkey, E. M. Costley, Haywood Pierce, Jr., J. Farmer, and W. Hugh McWhorter. Seated are (from left to right) Dr. Phillip G. Davison, J. Howell Green, J. Sam Guy, J. W. Battle, Leon Hollinsworth, Dr. Hamilton G. Ansley, and J. H. Kite. Sponsored by the Atlanta Rotary Club, the Decatur chapter has since sponsored clubs at Northlake and West DeKalb.

Bottom, left: Louise Trotti, right, served the DeKalb Library System from 1946 to 1981, becoming director in 1962. She is pictured with Donna Mancini, who served as director from 1991 to 1995.

Bottom, right: Barbara Loar, left, and Donna Mancini unveil a portrait of Loar on February 17, 1991. Loar, who served as director of the DeKalb Library System during the 1980s and '90s, was responsible for the opening of fifteen new library branches in DeKalb. She received a national award for creation of the Tobie Grant Homework Library, which provided after-school help for students in the Scottdale community.

Recuperating at Lawson General Hospital in Chamblee from war wounds that left his legs paralyzed, a young Clark Harrison wrote a newspaper column called "Chats from a Decatur GI." The column kept families in touch, by reporting about hometown "boys" and where they were serving during the war. Harrison served as chairman of the DeKalb Board of Commissioners from 1969 to 1972 and was a licensed pilot.

DeKalb's new water system, the brainchild of Commissioner Scott Candler, was finished in 1942 at a cost of $2 million. The system, and many other progressive achievements, had Candler mentioned as a gubernatorial candidate in 1945. Candler, however, continued to serve as county commissioner until 1954.

The years after World War II saw tremendous growth in DeKalb County. Returning soldiers were eager to settle down and begin families. New houses and apartments sprang up all over the county. Employment for the soldiers came from new industries, like General Motors' new Buick-Oldsmobile-Pontiac plant in Doraville. Dedicated in June, 1948 on 386 acres, the $7 million facility had a roof area

✧

Above: Clark Harrison not only was chairman of the DeKalb Board of Commissioners and a World War II hero, he also was a pilot. In 1987, he began a solo flight across the Atlantic in a 19-year-old single-engine Piper Cherokee 140 airplane guided by hand controls. The 64-year-old pilot, who was paralyzed from the chest down by a German sniper's bullet in World War II, fell short of his goal of Germany, crash landing in Greenland. He survived the rocky landing, thanks to some guidance from his friend, Pat Epps, who happened to be airborne at the same time, as well as from a higher source. When Harrison thought he might not make it, he began reciting the Twenty-third Psalm. Harrison later said that as he recited the line, "He maketh me lie down in green pastures," a green pasture appeared, giving him a safe place to land. Epps told this story in an article in the February 2006 issue of Business and Commercial Aviation *magazine.*

Right: DeKalb Peachtree Airport—inexplicably known as PDK—opened in 1959, after several failed attempts to convert the property into a county airport. DeKalb began preparations to acquire the old Camp Gordon property for a county airport as early as 1935, but the effort was interrupted by World War II, when it was commissioned as a U.S. Naval Air Station. By 1972, when this photo was taken, the airport was home to 300 aircraft. Today, the 765-acre facility houses 590 aircraft and is the second busiest airport in Georgia.

of seventeen acres and an assembly line capable of working on 550 cars at once. The plant is now scheduled for closure, and redevelopment of the large site is anticipated.

In the late 1940s DeKalb had 15 independent school districts, each with its own trustees and tax system. Most schools did not meet state standards, and many lacked heat or running water. A young man named Jim Cherry changed all that. On temporary assignment from the state Department of Education, he ran for county school superintendent and stayed in that job for 23 years. Under his leadership, DeKalb became one of the nation's best school systems. DeKalb Technical School opened in 1963, followed by DeKalb Community College, the only junior college in the nation operated by a local school system. The college became part of the University System of Georgia in 1997, and the name was changed to Georgia Perimeter College.

The 1940s also saw the arrival of Narvie Jordan Harris, one of the county's first supervisors of the Jeanes program operated by the Division of Negro Education of the Georgia Department of Education. Harris was considered the county's "black school superintendent" until integration in 1967. She served as Instructional Coordinator for Elementary Education until her retirement from the DeKalb School System in 1983.

During much of Harris' tenure, DeKalb schools operated under the supervision of federal courts, following a successful suit that claimed that the county maintained a segregated school system. DeKalb was declared by the courts to be successfully integrated in 1989.

The growth that began after World War II continued into the next decade, as DeKalb became the second fastest growing county in country between 1950 and 1960. Where dairy farms had consumed most of the land subdivisions sprang up, earning DeKalb the moniker of Atlanta's "bedroom community."

The Communicable Disease Center (now called Centers for Disease Control and Prevention), which began in 1946, started construction on a new facility on Clifton Road in 1956. The CDC played a key role in one of the greatest triumphs of public health: the worldwide eradication of smallpox.

The county's five-man county board of commissioners replaced the one-man system in 1957. The first commissioners were Chairman Claude H. Blount, Clark Harrison, Jr., Julian Harris, Charlie Parker, and J. W. Toney. DeKalb changed its form of government again in 1985, establishing the position of Chief Executive Officer, similar to the mayor of a municipality.

The late 1950s brought a new phenomenon to the county—the two-car family. Population projections for the metropolitan area for 1970 were exceeded before 1960, and road construction shifted into high gear, with such big projects as Buford Highway underway in 1957.

The DeKalb Grand Jury, in operation since the first days of the county, got its first African-American and female members in the 1950s. Clifford Payne became the first black member in 1952, and Ethel North the first woman three years later.

After 30 years in downtown Atlanta, the Henrietta Egleston Children's Hospital moved to the campus of Emory University in 1959. The hospital was the dream of Thomas R. Egleston, who was the only one of Henrietta's children to survive to adulthood. The first hospital in Georgia to perform a pediatric heart

transplant, Egleston completed a $25 million expansion in 1981. Egleston Children's Health Care System and Scottish Rite Children's Medical Center merged in 1998 to become Children's Healthcare of Atlanta.

The surge in population during the 1950s prompted DeKalb to seek support for a county hospital. The DeKalb County Hospital Authority was created in 1957. The first board members were Dr. Rufus Evans, Dr. James Ross McCain, Julius A. McCurdy, R. L. Mathis, Jr., W. W. Lively, Hugh A. Rowland, and M. E. Smith. The 200-bed DeKalb General Hospital (now DeKalb Medical Center) opened on 40 acres on North Decatur Road in 1961. DeKalb Medical also operates a hospital in downtown Decatur, as well as a hospital in Lithonia, which opened in 2005.

The twentieth century in DeKalb saw its share of notable citizens, but none so intriguing as Tobie Grant. Called "Aunt Tobie," she was born in 1887 in Scottdale of African-American and Indian ancestry. She owned an insurance company and considerable land in the community, but was known for her psychic abilities. She called herself a "sense-giver" or "adviser," and people came from miles around to hear her "advice." She is credited with finding missing persons, and she predicted use of atomic bomb more than a decade before it happened.

Before her death in 1968, Grant donated the land for the library, park, and recreation center that bear her name. Although she was far from ordinary, she is one of the few ordinary citizens to have facilities named after her.

The county's new courthouse opened in 1967, with the old granite courthouse used for offices until its restoration for use as headquarters of the DeKalb Historical Society and a special event facility.

Executive Park, possibly the nation's first all-office building park, opened in 1966 on 103 acres of the Lively dairy farm on North Druid Hills Road at I-85. Developer Mike Gearon envisioned "blue chip tenants" in buildings of "striking architecture" in a "sylvan setting." Debate abounded concerning the perceived threat to downtown Atlanta by suburban office complexes. That debate intensified as office developments, like Perimeter Center, sprawled to the edges of I-285 and

✧

As incongruous at it seems, lovely young women dressed in white bathing suits and high heels urged DeKalb residents to recycle rubber and metal, which were needed for fighting World War II. Note that the woman on the left is holding a rubber duck.

SPECIAL COLLECTIONS DEPARTMENT, GEORGIA STATE UNIVERSITY LIBRARY.

✧

The American Legion's scrap metal depository was on the grounds of the courthouse during World War II, conveniently located so that citizens could back up their trucks and unload old car parts and other metal scrap. Citizens were urged to recycle anything made of metal—from razor blades to pots and pans to garden fencing.

SPECIAL COLLECTIONS DEPARTMENT, GEORGIA STATE UNIVERSITY LIBRARY.

✧

In 1944, two years before this photo was taken, DeKalb had seventeen black schools with 1,500 students and 36 teachers. Schools were housed in churches and lodges and were funded in part by Anna T. Jeanes, a Quaker philanthropist from Pennsylvania. The Jeanes program was administered by the Division of Negro Education of the Georgia Department of Education. Integrated schools would not become a reality in DeKalb for more than 20 years after these children gathered on the steps of their school.

COURTESY OF THE SPECIAL COLLECTIONS DEPARTMENT, GEORGIA STATE UNIVERSITY LIBRARY.

✧

Agnes Scott College coeds are pictured in the school's library in 1945, more than 50 years after the school's founding. In proposing the idea for a school for women, founder George Washington Scott said that educating women would mean educating families. Agnes Scott College became a four-year, degree-granting institution in 1906.

SPECIAL COLLECTIONS DEPARTMENT, GEORGIA STATE UNIVERSITY LIBRARY.

✧

Top, left: Peachtree Industrial Boulevard was new in 1954, when construction began on the Frito-Lay factory. The road had been constructed specifically to access new industries that were being built in Chamblee and Doraville. The factory was a popular tour for school children, and long-time residents will remember tons of potatoes being dumped from tractor-trailer trucks into giant bins outside the loading docks. It was always easy to tell when it was pork rind day because of the aroma that filled the air. Lay's was demolished in the 1990s to make way for a home improvement store. One of the signs at left advertises steak for $1.50 per pound.

COURTESY OF THE SPECIAL COLLECTIONS DEPARTMENT, GEORGIA STATE UNIVERSITY LIBRARY

Top, right: The General Motors Assembly Division built a plant in a cow pasture in Doraville in 1947. By the early 1970s the facility had built its one millionth vehicle. Plant manager William Canning, left, is seen welcoming Governor Jimmy Carter to the official ceremony. The plant will close in 2008, depriving the city of Doraville of considerable revenue and leaving the 120-acre site ready for redevelopment.

Right: Jim Cherry came to DeKalb as a consultant on loan from the Georgia Department of Education and never left. He ran for school superintendent in 1948 and retired in 1972. When he first arrived, DeKalb had 15 school districts, each governed by a separate board of trustees. Many schools had no indoor plumbing and were heated by pot-bellied stoves. Within five years of his election, Cherry had unified county schools under one five-member board.

beyond. On one side of the debate was Gearon, developer of Perimeter Center, and on the other John Portman, developer of Peachtree Center. In the 1980s and into the 1990s, more and more residents from inside the Perimeter moved to exurban counties to escape the sprawl. But as the '90s came to a close, commuters tired of spending more and more time in their cars began to move back to suburban and urban neighborhoods. The revitalization of close-in communities also was driven by high gasoline prices and environmental concerns. These changes resulted in the new millenium's emphasis on mixed-use developments and live-work-play areas.

The 1970s began decades of advancement and achievement for women and minorities in DeKalb. Betty Clark became the first African-American woman elected to the state House of Representatives. Elected in 1973, she served until 1990. Liane Levetan became DeKalb's first female commissioner in 1974. John Evans was elected DeKalb's first black county commissioner in 1983.

In 1971, less than two years after suffering a devastating injury in Vietnam, Max Cleland took the oath of office as a state senator from Lithonia. He would go on to head the U.S. Veterans Administration at the age of 34, serve as Georgia secretary of state for 14 years, and to serve one term as U.S. senator.

A huge explosion and fire erupted in Doraville in the quiet, pre-dawn hours of April 6, 1972. An overfilled tanker truck at the gasoline storage facility sent fumes into the nearby Doral Circle neighborhood, where they came in contact with a furnace pilot light. The home exploded, and flames consumed several of the huge tanks. The homeowner and one Triangle Refineries

employee were killed. Flames could be seen in Alabama, The fire burned for four days, and volunteer firefighters came from all over the country to help fight the blaze. The incident resulted in an intense safety campaign by oil companies and public safety officials.

Although Hosea Williams already was well known as a civil rights leader, he first ran for public office from DeKalb in 1974. He served in the state Senate until 1985, after which his wife, Juanita, successfully ran for the office

✧

DeKalb's young people helped promote the sale of war bonds during World War II by riding in a decorated Jeep around Courthouse Square. Even children could participate in the effort to finance the war by purchasing treasury stamps for as little as ten cents. The small amounts could be used toward the purchase of an $18.75 bond, which could be redeemed in ten years for $25. The government's effort to raise money for the war also was carried to DeKalb living rooms via the radio, with celebrities like Roy Rogers delivering the message.

SPECIAL COLLECTIONS DEPARTMENT, GEORGIA STATE UNIVERSITY LIBRARY

✧

Pine Lake Police Chief Roy Purvis is pictured in 1960 with the town's only police car. Pine Lake, DeKalb's smallest municipality, was incorporated in 1937, after many years as a small subdivision. The community was created with cottages on small lots around a fishing lake as a weekend retreat for people who lived in faraway Atlanta. At the time of the 2000 U.S. census, Pine Lake had only 321 houses and 621 residents.

and served four terms. Hosea Williams subsequently served on the Atlanta City Council and the DeKalb Board of Commissioners. He died in 2000.

Two years after Hosea Williams successfully ran for the state Senate, a young Florida lawyer opened her practice in Decatur. In 1984, Carol Hunstein defeated four male candidates for a seat on the DeKalb Superior Court. She was appointed as only the second woman to serve on the Georgia Supreme Court in 1992. A polio and cancer survivor, Hunstein currently is the court's presiding justice. She serves with fellow DeKalb resident, George H. Carley.

The Metropolitan Atlanta Rapid Transit Authority began rail service through east and north DeKalb, when it opened the East Line between Georgia State University and Avondale in 1979. Stations on the East Line included Decatur, East Lake, and Edgewood-Candler Park. The Brookhaven Station on the North Line opened in 1984, followed by Chamblee in 1987. MARTA extended the East Line to Kensington and Indian Creek in 1993. A new branch to Dunwoody opened in 1996. DeKalb and Fulton voters approved the rail service in 1971, with an initial fare of 25 cents.

No one who lived through it will ever forget the early morning hours of Thursday, April 9, 1998. That is when a tornado ripped through Dunwoody's Chamblee Dunwoody-Peeler Road area and the Kingsley, Fontainebleu Forest, and Lockridge Forest

✧

Left: DeKalb's "new" courthouse opened in 1967 with a fountain in front. An addition behind this building, with all the latest security features, opened in 2006. The fountain has been replaced with landscaping.

Below: DeKalb Commission Chairman Manuel Maloof displaces a little turf while trying to hit a golf ball at the opening of Sugar Creek Golf Course in 1984. Located on Bouldercrest Road, the 18-hole public course is one of two operated by the DeKalb Parks and Recreation Department.

✧

Top, right: Thurbert Baker, pictured at the kickoff of his first campaign for state attorney general, was appointed to that office in 1997. He won election in 1998, 2002, and 2006. Baker served as a state representative from DeKalb from 1989 to 1997, during which time he was Governor Zell Miller's floor leader. Baker came to DeKalb to attend Emory University Law School after graduating from the University of North Carolina at Chapel Hill, where he was on the fencing team. He was Atlantic Coast Conference individual saber champion in 1979.

Top, left: When the Metropolitan Atlanta Rapid Transit Authority began construction of its East Line through Decatur in 1976, it met with a large obstacle—the Confederate monument on the grounds of the Old Courthouse. As it turned out, the obstacle was not so formidable after all. After raising the monument onto wooden rails, it took only one man to move the monument the few feet north necessary to accommodate the construction.

Bottom: On a cool, misty morning in April 1972, gasoline fumes from an over-filled tanker truck flowed from the Triangle Refineries facility in Doraville to the basement of a home on Doral Circle. The exploded home completely disintegrated, leaving nothing but this driveway. The resulting fire burned storage tanks for four days, bringing volunteer firefighters from across the nation.

subdivisions, causing one death and destroying 3,000 homes and 100,000 mature trees.

As soon as the storm had passed, the Dunwoody Homeowners Association, Dunwoody Preservation Trust, and the Dunwoody Nature Center pooled their resources and launched the Replant the Dunwoody Forest initiative. In the next three

years, they raised money and planted twenty-five thousand trees, according to a master plan by Roy Ashley. The effort educated homeowners about selection, planting, and care of new trees, and planted trees in many public spaces.

The biggest fundraiser was Feast of the Forest hosted by Holway's Coach House, which raised $35,000. The community celebrated the one-year anniversary of the tornado with an event that grew into the annual Lemonade Days festival. The all-volunteer project has been used as a model for other similar disaster recovery efforts.

Among the houses damaged was the historic Donaldson-Chesnut House on Chamblee Dunwoody, where many huge trees were destroyed. The home was repaired and the landscaping renovated. DeKalb County acquired the house, cemetery, and acreage in October 2005.

During the 1990s, DeKalb experienced a dramatic shift in demographics. According to U.S. census records, the county as a whole went from being majority white in 1990 to majority black in 2000. DeKalb Chamber of Commerce statistics show that DeKalb's white population decreased between 1990 and 2000 by almost 20 percent, while the African-American population increased by almost 57 percent.

During that same period, DeKalb's Hispanic population increased by 236 percent. The vast majority of that increase occurred in the Chamblee-Doraville area. The city of Chamblee went from having a Hispanic population of only 0.2 percent to being majority Hispanic. The city of Doraville went from having nearly one percent Hispanic residents to almost evenly split between white and Hispanic. Decatur became a bit more white during the '90s, with a slight increase in both Asian and Hispanic residents.

While DeKalb, especially Chamblee and Doraville, has many Asian-owned businesses, the resident Asian population is comparatively small. The county went from being three percent Asian in 1990 to only four percent in 2000. Nonetheless, DeKalb has the largest Chinese population in Georgia.

The stretch of Buford Highway between North Druid Hills Road and the Gwinnett County line is called the International Corridor. Within that stretch are hundreds of small businesses owned by Asian and Hispanic immigrants. Probably two of the best known concentrations of international businesses are the Plaza del Sol and the Chinatown Mall, both in the city of Chamblee. Chinatown Mall is located adjacent to the Chinese Community Center. After many years of planning, developers began work in early 2007 on the International Village. Located across Chamblee-Tucker Road from DeKalb Peachtree Airport, the mixed-use development will contain shops, restaurants, a hotel, a trade center, and an outdoor amphitheater.

Reflective of the population shift, Alvin T. Wong was elected as a State Court judge for DeKalb in 1998, becoming the first Asian-American judge in the Southeast.

The county's new diversity is reflected in the demographics of the school system. Students in DeKalb schools currently are 76 percent black, 10 percent white, 8 percent Hispanic, 3 percent Asian, and 3 percent of other races. In 2006, students represented 170 countries, from Afghanistan to Zimbabwe. By far the most students from outside the United States were natives of Mexico, followed by Ethiopia, Somalia, Jamaica, and India.

Students came from countries that most DeKalb citizens probably have never heard of, like Andorra in western Europe (between Spain and France), Guinea-Bissua in western Africa, and Seychelles, a nation of 115 islands in the Indian Ocean northeast of Madagascar. DeKalb students, in 2006, spoke 140 languages, including Spanish, but also languages like Adja, Armenian, Divehi, Ethiopian, Korean, Somali, and Twi.

Many of the students, especially in the Clarkston area, are members of refugee families, who fled the violence in their homelands.

In the new millennium DeKalb County is far removed from the sleepy country place it was from the 1870s to the 1940s or the "bedroom community" it became in the mid-twentieth century. More urban than suburban, it has not only a diverse population, but also a diverse economy and culture. DeKalb has changed to such an extent that pioneers like James Montgomery, Mary Gay, and Asa Candler probably would not recognize the places where they lived. But, these hardy souls would fit right in with today's thriving communities and businesses that are paving the way for DeKalb's future.

Above: The biggest event to hit Decatur since the Civil War was the Olympics in 1996. Huge crowds gathered as the torch made its way downtown. DeKalb had one sports venue—the tennis center at Stone Mountain Park. Athletes and guests from 197 nations attended the centennial Olympic games.

Left: DeKalb County has become increasingly diverse over the past two decades. At the center of that diversity is Emory University, which attracts students from all over the world. Margarita Parra with ten-month-old Dominique Regalado represented Paraguay at Emory University's International Cultural Festival of 1995.

PEOPLE, PLACES & EVENTS

✧ *Noted golfer Bobby Jones got his start as a youngster at East Lake Golf Club.*

BOBBY JONES

The Atlanta Athletic Club completed construction of a new seven-hole golf course in 1906 in East Lake, a popular resort for Atlanta's elite. The club would produce many talented golfers, but the best was Robert Tyre "Bobby" Jones, the greatest amateur golfer of all time.

Soon after Robert P. and Clara Thomas Jones moved their family, including a sickly Bobby, to their summer home near East Lake, the child began to thrive on sports. His favorites were baseball and golf. He never had formal lessons, just imitated adults using a hand-me-down club.

Jones won his first tournament in 1908 at the age of six. In 1911, at the age of nine, he defeated Howard Thorn, who was twice his age, to win the Atlanta Athletic Club junior title. The pinnacle of his remarkable career came in 1930 when he won all four major tournaments—the American Amateur, American Open, British Amateur, and British Open Tournament. Called the "grand slam," it is still considered one of the greatest achievements in sports.

"The Boy Wonder of East Lake" returned to Atlanta in 1930 to "one of the greatest parades ever witnessed in Atlanta," according to *The Atlanta Constitution*.

Jones shocked the golfing world when he retired from the sport at the age of 28. With a bachelor of science in mechanical engineering from Georgia Tech and a bachelor of arts in English literature from Harvard, he set his sights on a law degree. After one year at Emory Law School, he passed the bar exam and opened a law practice in Atlanta.

He went on to make eighteen golfing instructional films, and, working with A. G. Spalding and Company, designed the first matched set of golf clubs. For the first time the clubs were given numbers instead of names.

Jones was as good a golf course designer as he was a player. He designed Augusta National, which is considered one of the finest courses in the world. Augusta's Masters Tournament, first played in 1934, is one of four major tournaments played today.

In 1942, at the age of 40, Jones was commissioned a captain in U.S. Army Air Corps. He served in Europe and completed his service with the rank of lieutenant colonel.

Jones played his last round of golf in 1948, the year he was diagnosed with a rare and painful central nervous system disorder, which eventually confined him to a wheelchair. He died in 1971 in Atlanta at the age of 69 and is buried at Atlanta's Oakland Cemetery.

When asked about his fateful illness, Jones, ever the gentleman, said, "We all have to play the ball as it lies."

✧ *More than 230,000 U.S. Army soldiers—both infantry and artillery—were trained at Camp Gordon. Among the soldiers was Sgt. Alvin York, noted both for being a conscientious objector and a war hero. A popular movie was made about the Tennessee Medal of Honor winner.*

JOE LEE COLLECTION

CAMP GORDON

In 1917, at the height of World War I, hundreds of thousands of men invaded north DeKalb County. The invasion began with a scouting expedition in January. But these were not enemy soldiers. They were Americans getting ready to go to war.

Rejecting its previous stand of neutrality, the United States declared war on Germany in April of 1917. With the declaration came an increased urgency to train new soldiers fast in order to send them to the European front.

The U.S. Army was looking for acreage with access to a railroad, a good water supply, and level ground suitable for setting up rifle and artillery ranges. A 2,400-acre tract along the railroad in Chamblee was purchased in July from Atlanta Mayor Asa G. Candler. At the time the nearest water service was in the city of Atlanta, thirteen miles away. Mayor Candler advanced his personal funds in order for the water line to be run to the property. The Georgia legislature enacted a special "war tax" to repay Candler.

With water and rail transportation available, the U.S. Army began to transform the formerly peaceful farmland into an infantry and artillery training cantonment called Camp Gordon, named for Confederate general and Georgia governor John B. Gordon.

By July there was unprecedented activity in the area known as Old Cross Keys. *The Atlanta Journal* noted that the rolling acreage which held a small house or two and some clumps of trees was "transformed from calm stillness to hustle and bustle such as is seldom witnessed in a lifetime." Four thousand work men converged on the site to cut trees, lay roads and railroad spurs, and build barracks and mess halls. Buildings went up at a rate of eight per day in the new "army city." The finished camp included 1,635 buildings with barracks for 46,612 men and corral space for 7,688 horses and mules.

Chamblee was a tiny town, having been incorporated only nine years earlier. The city had only one main street a post office, railroad depot and two stores. By mid-August, 1917, there were forty stores, movie theaters, and two hotels. Everywhere there was red clay dust, people, mules, trucks, and automobiles. Every community activity was disrupted. Chamblee Baptist Church found itself at one entrance to the cantonment, and church-goers had to go through a checkpoint to attend services. Streetcar service inched its way toward the camp from the county line in Brookhaven, with the line completed more than a month after the camp actually opened.

The cantonment opened on September 5, and recruits poured in from Georgia, Alabama, and Tennessee. In all, 6,153 officers and 227,312 enlisted men trained at the camp. December of 1917 in Old Cross Keys was called the "Khaki Christmas."

The famed 328th Infantry, 82nd Division, American Expeditionary Force and the Emory University Medical Unit (Base Hospital 43) both served with distinction in France. Among the 82nd was the war's most decorated hero, Sgt. Alvin York of Tennessee. York's daring attack on an enemy machine gun position made him a hero and the subject of a movie. At least one soldier from each of the forty eight states served in the 82nd, earning it the nickname, the All-American Divisions. Members of this unit wear the distinctive AA patch today. DeKalb contributed 765 soldiers to war; eight never came home. One solder who did return was Maj. Scott Candler, who served as a company commander.

The war ended in November 1918, and the cantonment was abandoned as quickly as it was created.

There was interest in making a portion of the camp into an airport as early as the 1920s. The Atlanta Aero Club kept the idea alive, DeKalb County made plans to purchase 300 acres in 1940. The first private plane landed on a dirt runway in 1941, but the idea of a county airport stalled that same year, again because of a world war.

The federal government reclaimed the property for a Naval Air Station training facility for Navy pilots, and the 82nd Infantry was recommissioned the 82nd Airborne. For two years it was used for training Navy fighter pilots and flight instructors, as well as for a control tower operators' school. Lawson General Hospital also was build on the property. After the war, the Naval Air Station moved to Marietta, and the county finally had the clear opportunity to develop a public airport.

✧ *Epps Aviation began operation with a single hangar and nineteen employees at DeKalb Peachtree Airport in 1965. The company has continued to grow for the past forty years, adding a flight school in 1970, charter flights in 1971, and a new terminal in 1979.*

EPPS AVIATION

The new facility opened in 1959, with Henry F. "Doc" Manget as its first manag-

✧ *Pat Epps carries on the tradition begun by his father, Ben T. Epps, who built and flew an airplane in Athens in 1907, becoming the first pilot in Georgia. Ben's youngest son first soloed in 1952 and founded Epps Aviation in 1965. In 1992, Pat Epps completed an 11-year quest by rescuing one of the Lockheed P-38 Lightning aircraft that had been trapped beneath hundreds of feet of ice in Greenland since it crash landed with the rest of the Lost Squadron in 1942. Epps also flew a DC-3 to France in 1994 to celebrate the 58th anniversary of D-Day.*

EPPS AVIATION

er. Manget trained as a Navy pilot at the Naval Air Station in 1941. He served two combat tours in the Southwest Pacific, earning three Distinguished Service Crosses, among his many citations for valor. He was recalled to active service during the Korean War. He retired in 1990 after 31 years as airport manager. The airport recently dedicated the first aviation park in Georgia to Davis.

Although its official name is DeKalb Peachtree Airport (PDK), it is popularly called PDK. The second busiest airport in Georgia, it is home to almost 600 aircraft, including fifty corporate aircraft, and has an annual economic impact on the county of nearly $100 million. Almost 250,000 flights begin or end at PDK every day.

The airport currently consists of 765 acres and is home to corporate flight departments and to several aviation service companies. The best known is Epps Aviation. The company was started in 1965 and is still run by Pat Epps, son of Ben T. Epps, the first pilot in Georgia. Ben Epps built his first plane in 1907, and built five more before his death in a plane crash in 1937. The Athens airport is named in his honor.

At the age of 73, Pat Epps is well known for flying his aerobatic Beechcraft Bonanza in air shows, including the popular PDK Neighbor Day held every June. In 1981, Epps led an expedition to rescue one of eight World War II P-38s that crash landed in a blizzard in Greenland in 1942. A second expedition in 1992 rescued a P-38 Lightning buried 265 feet below the Greenland ice cap. His eleven-year quest is documented in his book, *The Lost Squadron*. In 1994, Epps flew a DC-3 to France to participate in the fiftieth anniversary of the Normandy Invasion.

✧ *On June 3, 2006, DeKalb Peachtree Airport opened the only aviation park in Georgia and dedicated a plaque to the airport's first manager, H. F. "Doc" Manget. Manget was assigned to the Naval Air Station in Chamblee after joining the Navy in 1941. He served two combat tours in the southwest Pacific during World War II and was operating from the* USS Princeton *when it was sunk during the Battle of Leyte Gulf in 1944. He was recalled to duty during the Korean conflict, and earned three Distinguished Flying Crosses for valor in combat in the two wars. Manget was the airport manager from 1959 to 2000. On hand for the ceremony was Toy Manget (pink shirt), who made her own mark on the county in various roles at the DeKalb Library System.*

✧ *Asa Griggs Candler is best known as the founder of the Coca-Cola Company. A large portion of the millions he made in the soft drink business were poured into projects in DeKalb County. Candler was the developer of the Druid Hills subdivision and the first benefactor of Emory University.*

MANUSCRIPT, ARCHIVES, AND RARE BOOK LIBRARY, EMORY UNIVERSITY

CANDLERS

According to one account of the Candler family, "No more distinguished family has been produced by the South. It has taken a position of leadership in affairs of finance, law, and religion." A 1910 publication noted, "Energy, intelligence, courage and probity are characteristics of the family." All of the seven sons of Samuel Charles Candler and Sarah Beall, were involved in business, government, and philanthropy.

Four chose to make DeKalb County their home. Milton Anthony Candler, John Slaughter Candler, Asa Griggs Candler, and Warren Akin Candler would make their mark on the entire Atlanta area. DeKalb County was forever changed by the Candler family.

Eldest son Milton was the first to settle in DeKalb, moving to Decatur from Cartersville in 1857. He married Decatur's Eliza Caroline Murphey and joined his father-in-law's law practice. Milton served in both the state House and Senate during Reconstruction and in the U.S. House from 1875-1879. At one time, Milton served in the state legislature with his father, Samuel, and his uncle, Ezekiel S. Candler.

Milton and Eliza had twelve children, one being Charles Murphey Candler. Murphey Candler practiced law and served in both the Georgia House and Senate. He and his wife, Mary Hough Scott, daughter of Agnes Scott College founder George Washington Scott, were parents of George Scott Candler.

✧ *Milton Anthony Candler was the eldest of the four Candler brothers who settled in DeKalb. An attorney, he served in the state legislature and was a U.S. representative from 1875 to 1879. He was the grandfather of DeKalb's famous commissioner Scott Candler.*

MANUSCRIPT, ARCHIVES, AND RARE BOOK LIBRARY, EMORY UNIVERSITY

Asa Griggs Candler, the eighth child of this family, is best known as the founder of the Coca-Cola Company, but he also was a banker, real estate developer, and philanthropist. Candler's $2,300 invest-

✧ *Warren Akin Candler, 10 years younger than his brother Milton, was a bishop in the Southern Methodist Episcopal Church. He became the first chancellor of Emory University when the school moved to DeKalb in 1914.*

MANUSCRIPT, ARCHIVES, AND RARE BOOK LIBRARY, EMORY UNIVERSITY

ment to purchase the soft drink formula in 1888 made him a millionaire by 1920.

Candler was involved in two significant real estate deals that changed the face of DeKalb County. Candler purchased land to the east of Atlanta in 1908 from developer Joel Hurt. Under Candler's leadership, the development became the Druid Hills subdivision. Candler subsequently purchased acreage now bounded by Clairmont Road, Buford Highway, and Dresden Drive from a struggling farmer named Harwell Parks Tilly, who abandoned the area for more fertile land in south Georgia. When the United States government came looking in 1917 for land on which to build an army training camp, Candler sold the property. Because no local government had the funds necessary to run water and sewer lines to the property, he then made large personal loans to finance the necessary infrastructure.

Asa moved from his home, called Callan Castle, in Inman Park to a new mansion in his Druid Hills subdivision in 1916. Land in Druid Hills donated by Candler provided the site for Emory University's move from Oxford, Ga. to Atlanta. Asa was the major benefactor of Emory during the early years after the move. His gifts totaled almost $8 million. He gave the last of his fortune to Emory in the mid-1920s. In 1922, the *Carroll County* [Georgia] *Times* newspaper called Asa Candler "the South's richest man."

Asa had arrived in Atlanta on July 7, 1873, at the age of 21, with $1.75 in his pocket, having just completed an apprenticeship as a druggist in Cartersville. By 9 p.m. on his first day in town, he had landed a job in the drug store of George J. Howard on Peachtree Street. He worked until the store closed at midnight that night. He later married the boss's daughter, Lucy Howard. His impact on Atlanta and DeKalb during the next 56 years is incalculable.

John Slaughter Candler was the eleventh child, but the first to move to his brother Asa's Druid Hills subdivision. He taught school in DeKalb, then joined the law firm of Candler and Thomson, where his older brother, Milton, was a senior member. He later served as solicitor-general of the Stone Mountain Circuit, then Superior Court judge. In 1902 he was elected associate justice of the Georgia Supreme Court, but resigned four years later due to ill health. After his resignation, he rejoined the law firm.

John also raised prize Guernsey cattle at a "gentleman's dairy farm" he built in 1900 on Covington Highway called Mileybright Farm. John was a charter member of the Druid Hills Methodist Church.

Warren and John died three months apart in 1941. Of the four brothers, Asa lived the longest, dying in 1953. Milton, a semi-invalid, died in 1909.

✧ *John Slaughter Candler was the youngest of DeKalb's four Candler brothers. His was the first house to be built in his brother's Druid Hills Subdivision. He was an associate justice on the Georgia Supreme Court from 1902 to 1906.*

MANUSCRIPT, ARCHIVES, AND RARE BOOK LIBRARY, EMORY UNIVERSITY

Aside from Asa, no single member of this distinguished family had a larger impact on DeKalb County than George Scott Candler, son of Charles Murphey Candler and Mary Scott. He was mayor of Decatur when he easily defeated three opponents to become the county's sole Commissioner of Roads and Revenues. During the post-war boom years, Scott Candler was the architect of many milestones of progress, including developing the county's infrastructure.

The new county water system, which began operating in 1942, was the first county-operated water system south of Virginia. Other initiatives that began during Candler's administration include improvements to sewers, police, fire and sanitation service, libraries, and parks. His leadership also made possible the first county hospital and the DeKalb Peachtree Airport.

The trio of Candler, county attorney Julius McCurdy, and executive assistant Leon "Country" O'Neal were more than a match for any issue that arose in the county.

The infrastructure improvements enabled Candler to lure industries such as General Motors to the county. As Candler closed the deal with the General Motors official in 1947, the official asked when the county commission would meet to approve the deal. Candler replied, "We've met and I voted 'yes.' I'm it." In all, Candler brought 68 industrial complexes to the county between 1939 and 1966.

The 1945 grand jury presentments said, "On all sides during our inspection of various affairs in the county we found evidence of the value of his [Candler's] handiwork, evidence of his farsightedness, of his diligence, of his scrupulous fairness, his abounding energy, his ability to get things done, his sound judgment in his administration of affairs and of his unquestioned personal integrity."

The Atlanta Journal said, "His enemies call him a dictator, but his supporters say he's nearly always right. And when he decides a thing should be done, it never occurs to him that it can't be done." During Candler's tenure, DeKalb grew into Georgia's second most populous county and the wealthiest in the Southeast. He was affectionately known as "Mr. DeKalb."

As manager of the Stone Mountain Authority from 1959 to 1963 and state Secretary of Commerce, he laid the groundwork for completion of the Confederate memorial carving, creating a 3,800-acre park to showcase the memorial.

Descendants of the various branches of the Candler family are active in Atlanta and DeKalb County affairs today.

CHURCHES

As soon as settlers finished their houses—and sometimes before—they built the churches that would be the center of community life. In the first few years of the county's existence new churches sprang up in every corner of the county.

Baptists and Methodists—the so-called "frontier religions"—generally were the first to organize, followed closely by Presbyterians. Other denominations and religions came later in the county's development.

However, before there were organized congregations, religious duties were handled by ministers from the Ocmulgee Association of the Baptist Church. At a convention in 1823, sixteen ministers agreed to spend weeks in itinerant labor in Georgia's new counties, including DeKalb. The following year DeKalb's first two churches applied for membership in the new Yellow River Association.

DeKalb's first Methodist circuit rider, Morgan Bellah, was expected to preach in every neighborhood in the Decatur and to promote camp meetings—all for the paltry sum of $180 per year. He once said he overheard two men comment on the rider's salary, saying that the preacher "ought to have at least as much as an ordinary field hand."

Macedonia Baptist Church on Panola Road in south DeKalb was the first to organize. Constituted as a Primitive Baptist church in 1823, it is still in operation in its original location. Huge old cedar trees shade the cemetery, where burials are still conducted. Church minutes, still in existence, show that members were required to address each other as "Brother" and "Sister."

Nancy Creek Primitive Baptist Church, organized in 1824, was the county's second church. Services are still held in the small brick church on Eighth Street in Chamblee. Since it was the first community cemetery in the area, it was the last resting place for many early north DeKalb residents, whether or not they were church members.

The creek, originally called Nance's Creek, was named for Nancy Baugh Evins, wife of John Leroy Evins, who is said to have preferred fishing to housework. Other early residents of the area known as Cross Keys included the Johnston, Evins, Coker, Wells, Jarrell, Holbrook, Spruill, Goodwin, and Flowers families.

Soon after the Baptists organized their little church in north DeKalb, the

✧ *Sylvester Baptist Church in southeast Atlanta appears almost ghostly in this photo taken about 1910. Organized in October of 1883, the church was named for Sylvester Terry, who died suddenly in 1872 at the age of 16. The Terry family experienced more than its share of tragedy. Thomas Terry, Sylvester's father, was murdered in Atlanta in 1861. His mother, Mary Jane Thurman Terry, donated the land for the church. Sylvester Cemetery is one of the oldest cemeteries in DeKalb. The congregation disbanded in 1972. Thirty years later neighbors and descendants of those buried in the cemetery began a massive cleanup effort and formed a foundation for its continuing care.*

DENNIS TAYLOR

Methodists followed suit. In 1826, Prospect Methodist constructed the first sanctuary in DeKalb, located where the Peachtree Indian trail (Peachtree Road) intersected with the Shallow Ford Trail, where today the Chamblee and Doraville city boundaries meet. The church's 1885 sanctuary, adjacent to the cemetery on Peachtree Road, now houses an antique store. The church changed its name to First United Methodist Church of Chamblee and moved into a new sanctuary on Chamblee Dunwoody Road in 1967.

Prosperity Associate Reformed Presbyterian Church opened its doors in

1836 just a few hundred yards up Peachtree Road from the Methodist church. Their respective cemeteries separated the two sanctuaries. Prosperity changed its name to Doraville Associate Reformed Presbyterian Church and moved into the heart of the city in 1872.

All three churches had many members who were prominent in the community and the county. These pioneers left behind their names on streets and other local landmarks. As in other areas of the county, their children intermarried and formed the backbone of the new county. Some descendants still live in the county today. Among those early north DeKalb settlers were the House, Tilly, McElroy, Flowers, Lively, and Akins families.

Down along Utoy Creek, in the extreme southwestern portion of the county, Utoy Primitive Baptist Church was organized in 1824. Early congregations disciplined their members for failing to attend, as well as for drunkenness, fighting, and other misconduct. One Utoy member was tossed out of the congregation for moving across the nearby Chattahoochee River into Indian country, which was illegal at the time.

No one knows the exact date of the founding of Hardman's (sometimes spelled Hardeman's) Meeting House. William Towers wrote in the church minute book that there were 15 members, including himself, on November 19, 1825. He reported that Hardman's sister churches were "Yallow River, Nance's Creek, Massadony, Cool Spring, Uty, and Fellowship."

Revolutionary veterans must have found Tucker a particularly congenial place to settle. Peter Cash, Daniel Fones, Edward Leavell, and Graner Whitley and their extended families organized Fellowship Primitive Baptist Church on August 15, 1829. The veterans, as well as other Tucker pioneers, are buried in the adjacent cemetery.

On July 18, 1834, Utoy church "took up the charge against Thomas Ray for fornication." The minutes recorded that Ray was found guilty and "ex'd" (excommunicated). The same year charges were heard against Willis Robuck for intemperence and Jeps Cox for "leaving this county without having paid his just debts." R. C. Todd was disciplined for "being frequently intoxicated and shooting."

✧ *Dr. Louie Newton raised sheep in his backyard in the fashionable Druid Hills neighborhood in the 1980s. The work of an itinerant sheepshearer Newton hired every spring is evident in this photo. Newton died at the age of 94 in 1986, one year after this photo was taken. He retired in 1969 after forty years as pastor of the Druid Hills Baptist Church. He served as president of the Southern Baptist Convention from 1947 to 1948, and founded Americans for Separation of Church and State in 1943.*

The most unusual case involved Bro. H. H. Embry. Mr. Embry came before the conference to charge himself "with having acted improperly by indirectly betting on an election." He sold a horse to a man, who would only be required to pay for the animal if Van Buren was elected president.

In one of DeKalb's oldest communities, Rock Chapel, a Methodist church was consecrated in 1825. The church was called the Soap Factory because of an old ash hopper on the grounds. The Bond, Diamond, Evans, Chupp, McGuffey, Griffin, Lee, Turner, Wellborn, Wesley, Marbut, Starnes, Johnson, Braswell, Cleland, Corley, and Ragsdale families attended the church. People came from miles around to take part in the popular camp meetings held at Rock Chapel. Former slaves who attended the church purchased the original building in 1866 and formed a separate church.

Wesley Chapel Methodist moved from Henry to DeKalb in 1828. An early sanctuary, along with the original church cemetery, are located at the intersection of Wesley Chapel and Snapfinger roads in south DeKalb.

One of the DeKalb Inferior Court's (today's county commission) first actions was to grant the Baptists, Methodists, and Presbyterians each a town lot in the city of Decatur on which to build a church.

The Presbyterians were the first to take advantage of the offer. In his speech, "An Historical Address," given on the occasion of the county's centennial celebration, Charles Murphey Candler gives the organization date of Decatur Presbyterian Church as 1825. The Reverend John S. Wilson organized the church, the oldest Presbyterian congregation in the county.

Early members of Decatur Presbyterian Church had to obtain "tokens of good standing" in order to partake of communion. As one came to the Communion table, he or she was required to surrender this token, a round piece of lead.

Decatur Methodist Church built its first sanctuary on Sycamore Street in 1826. The structure was the first church building in Decatur. The official constitution date for Decatur Baptist Church is November 21, 1862, although the church is thought to be considerably older.

Decatur's Civil War heroine, Mary Gay, helped raise funds for a building for Decatur Baptist. The Baptist Church of Decatur while in conference on August 24, 1867, reported: "We agreed, unanimously, to send our worthy Sister, Miss Mary A. H. Gay, out on a mission to solicit contributions, to aid us towards building a house to worship in. May the prayers

✧ *Mr. and Mrs. John Burnett, Sr. were the subject of this lovely, hand-made memorial. Mother Hannah Burnett was the founder of Lilly Hill Baptist Church in Decatur. The church began in the Burnett home on East Lake Drive, but rapidly outgrew the location. The church later moved to a building known as the Spring House near Atlanta Avenue and Water Street in Decatur.*

of the Church ever accompany her while absent from home, among strangers in so great an undertaking… May all good people assist her. May our heart be made to rejoice on her return of her success."

Members of the congregation had raised $600, not enough to build a church. During the next two years Mary Gay traveled around the South, collecting enough donations for a ample building fund. The first meeting in the little red brick church was held in 1871. The old church was replaced in 1926. Stained glass windows honored Mary Gay, who made it possible.

At its annual meeting in 1838, the Yellow River Association reported quite an increase in the number of Baptist churches in DeKalb. Indian Creek was organized the next year, but was burned by Sherman's soldiers during the Civil War. In response to a letter from Joseph Walker, a woman from the North paid to have the church rebuilt, at a cost of $325.

In its formative years, churches thrived in Atlanta alongside brothels and barrooms. Irish laborers, brought to Atlanta to work on the railroad, organized the Church of the Immaculate Conception (Roman Catholic) in 1848. Episcopalians, in 1849, completed St. Philip's, a small frame structure with a modest tower in what is now the Buckhead area of Fulton County. Decatur's first Episcopal church, Holy Trinity, was established in 1892. The church has sponsored three missions: St. Michael and All Angels, St. Bartholomew's and Holy Cross.

Additional Catholic, Episcopalian and other Protestant denominations, as well as Jewish congregations, came along later in the history of the county.

In 1854, Rehoboth Baptist Church trustees contracted with John Bolen Johns to construct a church building on Lawrenceville Highway near Tucker. The original contract, still owned by the church, called for the building to be 40 feet long and 30 feet wide, with four "batten doors," each six and one-half feet high and three and one-half feet broad, 12 side windows and an additional window behind the pulpit. The cost was set at $119. A youngster named Lester Buice was baptized there in 1933. He grew up to become the church's pastor in 1947. Rehoboth also grew, becoming at one time the county's largest church.

Hardman Primitive Baptist and Rock Chapel Methodist were the only two antebellum churches in the county that held separate services for slaves. Among Rock Chapel's black members was Hanna Weaver, who was a life-long member until her death in 1903. Slaves were allowed to sit in the balconies during white services at some other churches but were not permitted to hold their own separate services.

Shortly after the Civil War, Joseph Walker, a white man, organized Mt. Pleasant Baptist Church, the county's first black church. Walker deeded the land and a building to the church's first deacons and served as the pastor for a time. The church is still standing in its original location off Covington Highway on Porter Road.

Considered to be the oldest African-American church in Decatur, Antioch African Methodist Episcopal Church was the first in DeKalb to be founded exclusively by former slaves. Organized in 1868 in the home of Sister Lou Bratcher, the congregation built a one-room structure in 1874 on land on Trinity Street where the Callaway Building stands today. The congregation grew so fast that tickets had to be issued for services. Several influential Decatur residents, including Mrs. Annie Chewning and Virginia Washington, were members. The church sponsored recreational activities when no other opportunities existed in the community.

Another Antioch church, this one of the Baptist denomination, traces its official organization to 1911, but its roots are said to go back to 1867. The Reverend J. C. Center was the first pastor of the church, located on Old Covington Highway. He preached there for 45 years.

Mt. Zion African Methodist Episcopal Church was established in 1870 under the leadership of the Reverend Grannison Daniel. The church was first located near Lawrenceville Highway and called Rocky Knoll AME. An old railroad boxcar served as the first sanctuary and was located on land given by Judson Stokes. The church moved to its current location at 2977 LaVista Road in the 1890s.

Redan First Baptist Church, first known as Woodville Baptist, was organized in 1871 with 14 charter members. The area now known as Redan in southeast DeKalb was first called McCarter's Station for K. F. McCarter who donated the right of way for the Georgia Railroad. Reed Alford operated one of the first stores in the community. His wife's name was Annie. The town name is a combination of the first names of Mr. and Mrs. Alford.

The Reverend William Tillman, pastor of Atlanta's Wheat Street Baptist Church, organized Greater Travelers Rest Baptist

Church (not to be confused with Travelers Rest) in 1876. Sam Stinson and others who lived on the McDonough Road about three miles outside the Decatur town limits had been conducting Sunday school work in the area for several months. Stinson also conducted weekly prayer meetings. The church chose its name because it first met in a building that had been used as a resting place by Union soldiers on their way through Atlanta in 1864. The church has moved several times over the years, most recently to Tilson Road near Decatur in 1973. Early in its existence, the congregation refused a gift of land from Governor Joe Brown, choosing instead to buy a half-acre lot for $98 and to retain total control of the church property.

The Greater Mt. Carmel African Methodist Episcopal Church was started in the late 1870s by the Reverend George Washington Gholston. Meetings were first held at the Gholston home on Chamblee Tucker Road in what is now the Embry Hills community. The congregation later rented the Odd Fellows Lodge Hall on New Peachtree Road in Doraville, then Barrett's store on New Peachtree. A school for black children also met at Barrett's store. Mary J. Gholston was the first teacher.

Land for a cemetery was obtained in 1888 a short distance north of town on New Peachtree at Winters Chapel. In 1912 the church built its first sanctuary, adjacent to the cemetery, from timber cut on the Gholston property. The church next moved to property now occupied by the General Motors plant. Construction of the plant forced the church to move to its current location on Carver Circle in about 1961.

A group of Augusta residents moved to Decatur and in 1882 founded Thankful Baptist, the city's oldest black church. The Reverend Leon Tucker was the first full-time minister of the church, which has met over the years in several locations in the city. Organizers included Robert Tanksley, the Reverend Frank Paschal, Kittie House, Reese Howlworth, and the Reverend Lewis Thornton. The Reverend Martin Scruggs was the first pastor.

✧ *Flat Rock Methodist Church, shown with an inset of the Rev J. W. Queen, is the centerpiece of the black community at Flat Rock, located along the South River near Lithonia. Flat Rock dates back to the beginnings of the county, when Revolutionary soldier Joseph Emanuel Lyon and his family settled there. Today, Flat Rock is considered one of the oldest continuously-inhabited black communities in Georgia. Theodore A. Bryant, Sr. is credited with keeping encouraging black citizens to stay in Flat Rock during the Jim Crow years. The community recently was featured on a PBS program which traced the ancestry of nine African Americans, including comedian Chris Tucker. Tucker is the great great grandson of Eliza Waits, the common ancestor for many Flat Rock citizens. Members of the community recently opened the Flat Rock Archive center, with the goal of collecting and preserving information on African-American families and culture in DeKalb and protecting black cemeteries. Descendants of both white and black original settlers still live in the area.*

Thankful clerk D. G. Ebster recalled in his 1926 history of the church that, although the church had an organ, the congregation preferred to sing shaped notes and the old favorite hymns like *Amazing Grace* without accompaniment.

In his history Ebster also related stories about attending the school operated by Thankful Baptist. Children sat on benches and boxes and used blue-back spellers, slates, and pencils purchased by parents. Spelling was a highly-prized skill. Children considered themselves "professional spellers," if they could correctly spell "comprestibility."

At the turn of the twentieth century, "Mother" Hannah Burnett was a prominent religious leader in the East Lake community. By 1913 a large group of worshippers was meeting at her home on East Lake Drive. Hannah and John Burnett raised eleven children in that small house. On church meeting days, beds were moved into one part of the house to make room for chairs for the congregants. The church started by Mother Burnett was named Lilly Hill Baptist by Felix Banks. A Sunday school also met at the Burnett house, with Sister Roberta Watkins the first teacher. When the congregation outgrew the Burnett house, it met in a tent until a permanent church building was acquired.

The Greek Orthodox Cathedral of the Annunciation came to its DeKalb County home on Clairmont Road in 1964. The church began holding services in 1905 in rented space in downtown Atlanta. The cathedral's popular Greek Festival brings thousands of visitors to enjoy food and entertainment every fall.

DeKalb has six synagogues, the oldest being Beth Jacob on LaVista Road. The Marcus Jewis Community Center in Atlanta operates the popular Zaban Park in Dunwoody.

The relatively recent phenomenon of the "mega church" first came to DeKalb in the form of Chapel Hill Harvester, located on Flat Shoals Parkway. In its heyday in the 1980s, the church drew thousands to its services, which were well known for their eclectic style and use of contemporary music. Now named the Cathedral at Chapel Hill, the church is still operated by the Paulk family.

But, Chapel Hill pales in comparison to the New Birth Missionary Baptist Church.

Travelers Rest Baptist Church was organized in 1939 in the Scottdale community. A portion of the congregation moved in 1984 to a new location on Snapfinger Road in Lithonia and called itself New Birth. The calling of the Reverend Eddie Long to be the pastor three years later began a period of unprecedented growth for any church in the history of DeKalb.

In 1991, the church built a new $2 million sanctuary. By 1992, the congregation had outgrown the facility, growing from 300 members to 8,000. The church purchased 170 acres of land in 1996 and sold it a year later for an $11 million profit. With the proceeds, the church purchased 240 acres on Woodrow Road in Lithonia. Membership continued to grow, topping 25,000 in 2000.

New Birth moved into a $50 million dollar complex in the spring of 2001. The sanctuary seats 10,000 people. Auxiliary buildings contain administrative offices, a school, a library, bookstore, a computer lab, and audio and video studios. New Birth since has established churches in Atlanta, Jonesboro, Marietta, Charlotte, N. C., and Glen Allen, Va.

Eddie Long, consecrated the third presiding bishop in the Full Gospel Baptist Church Fellowship in 1994, is well known around the world and hosts a weekly television show. The church's Easter services at the Georgia Dome attract tens of thousands of worshippers. Bishop Long and the church are noted for their community activism and missions around the world.

Civil Rights

Compared to cities in Alabama and even Atlanta, the Civil Rights Movement in DeKalb County was remarkably quiet, although one local incident may have changed the course of the entire nation.

DeKalb actually was a bit ahead of its time. African American Clifford Payne served on the DeKalb Grand Jury in 1952, two years before the landmark Supreme Court decision on the *Brown vs. Board of Education* case. By comparison, Ethel North, the first woman on the Grand Jury, was appointed in 1955. The DeKalb Chapter of the National Association for the Advancement of Colored People (NAACP) was organized in 1956.

A simple traffic stop near Decatur may have influenced the outcome of the 1960 presidential election between John F. Kennedy and Richard Nixon. In May, 1960, Dr. Martin Luther King. Jr., newly moved from Alabama to Atlanta, was stopped by DeKalb police and cited for not having a Georgia driver's license. He was fined $25 and placed on probation for a year. Five months later he was arrested after a sit-in protest at the whites-only lunch counter at Rich's in downtown Atlanta. His probation was revoked, and he was sentenced to four months at the state prison in Reidsville. Intervention by the Kennedy family is said to have caused DeKalb Superior Court Judge Oscar Mitchell to set bond pending an appeal. The Georgia Court of Appeals overturned the sentence in 1961, and Judge Mitchell subsequently suspended the sentence.

The Kennedy family's involvement in King's release is said to have influenced black voters and helped Kennedy defeat Nixon by 100,000 votes, the closest presidential election in American history.

Locally, African Americans also had the support of a white Decatur citizen. In 1961 Frances Freeborn Pauley became the director of the Georgia Council on Human Relations. She later was a civil rights specialist for the U.S. Department of Health, Education, and Welfare. During her long career, Pauley's contributions to civil rights in the county ranged from school desegregation to voting. Pauley's remarkable career also included the war on poverty. She pioneered hot lunches in public schools, and in 1975, at the age of 67, she founded the Georgia Poverty Rights Organization.

Elizabeth Wilson was a young mother in Decatur in 1962. As African Americans, her children were not allowed to use public libraries. They had access to books only from the library at the black Trinity High School and from occasional bookmobile visits. Wilson and another mother, Dorothy Scott, were not trying to make a political statement or generate publicity. They had no plan and no high-profile backing. They simply wanted their children to have a better education. So they walked into the Decatur Library on Sycamore Street and gathered about a half dozen children's books. Sally Daniels waited outside in her car, in case there was trouble. After filling out the paperwork to obtain a library card, Wilson and Scott were allowed to borrow the books. Two years later, all public facilities throughout the county were integrated.

✧ *The city of Decatur dedicated a statue called* Celebration *to Mayor Emerita Elizabeth Wilson, left, on May 16, 2000. Among those attending the ceremony were former First Lady Rosalynn Carter and Decatur Mayor Bill Floyd. The statue, paid for by citizen contributions, is located on the Roy Blount, Sr. MARTA Plaza in downtown Decatur.*

ELIZABETH WILSON

Integrating the county's first public facility was just that easy. Desegregating Decatur schools took a little longer.

The U.S. Supreme Court ruled in 1955 that school boards would desegregate public schools "with all deliberate speed." In 1962 there were still no integrated schools in DeKalb. Elizabeth Wilson and Sadie Sims thought summer school might be a good way to begin the process. They went to Decatur School Superintendent Dr. Carl

Refroe to ask if their children might be allowed to attend the white summer session. Renfroe said no and advised that, if black parents wanted summer school for their children, they would have to hire teachers, find a location, and buy books.

A two-woman sit-in ensued, with neither side giving in or leaving the superintendent's office. By late afternoon, Dr. Renfroe had agreed to approach the school board. The board agreed to organize summer school for black children. Wilson knows what the effort meant to DeKalb's black school children, but what she remembers most about the day was that she was four months' pregnant and needed a restroom visit in the worst way.

City schools were not fully integrated for another two years, at which time the city's black schools closed. County schools were desegregated in 1967.

Wilson's son, Richard, was the first African American to attend Decatur High School. Her son, Carter, currently is athletic director and basketball coach there.

Wilson went on to significant accomplishments in Decatur. She founded the Oakhurst Community Health Center in the 1970s, which began as the tiny Beacon Clinic. When Wilson retired in 1994, the center had six physicians and provided complete primary care for families. She became the first African American elected to the Decatur City Commission in 1983 and was elected the first African-American mayor 10 years later. She retired as mayor in 1999. The "Celebration" statue on the Roy Blount Sr. MARTA Plaza was dedicated to Wilson in 2000.

Elizabeth Wilson has won just about every award DeKalb has to offer, including the county History Maker Award. In honor of that award, Decatur High established a scholarship in her name.

Once the civil rights movement got rolling, "firsts" rapidly occurred in all parts of the county. Willard Strickland and R. A. Knight became the first African-American police officers in Decatur in 1964. James Dean became the first black member of the state House of Representatives in 1966. Eugene C. Maner, Jr. became the first black to hold an administrative position in DeKalb government in 1968. Allison Venable was elected to the Lithonia City Council in 1973; he later would be mayor.

✧ *Five DeKalb County officials performed Motown hits by The Temptations at a 1991 benefit for the United Negro College Fund. Putting on a show are lead singer Thomas Brown and, from left to right, Dr. Melvin Johnson, Dr. Thomas Coleman, Vernon Jones, and Dr. Eugene Walker. Brown currently is DeKalb's sheriff. Jones is the county's chief executive officer. Walker is chairman of the Economic Development Authority of DeKalb County. During his eight years as a state senator from DeKalb (1984-1992), Walker was the first African-American Majority Whip.*

William C. Brown became the first African American on the DeKalb Library System Board in 1976; he would become chairman and serve on the DeKalb Board of Commissioners. John Evans became the first black county commissioner in 1983, and Phil McGregor the first black Board of Education member in 1983. McGregor also served as school board chairman. In 1986 Eugene Walker was elected the first black state senator since Reconstruction. Linda Hunter was the county's first black trial judge, elected in 1987.

African Americans continued their advancement in public life in the 1990s, with Thomas E. Brown as fire chief, then director of public safety; Jeanette Rozier, clerk of Superior Court; Thurbert Baker as state attorney general; Chuck Burris, mayor of Stone Mountain; Juanita Baranco, chairman of the Georgia Board of Regents (governing body of the state university system); and Vernon Jones, DeKalb's chief executive officer.

The first African American to represent Georgia in the U.S. House of Representatives was Cynthia McKinney of Stone Mountain. She served from 1993 to 2003 and from 2005 to 2007.

DeKalb County also was home to one of the civil rights movement's most influential and often controversial leaders.

Hosea Williams left his home in Decatur County at age 14. He served in an all-black unit in the U.S. Army during World War II. A severe wound left him with a life-long limp. He earned his high school diploma at age 23 and a chemistry degree from Morris Brown College. He and his wife, Juanita Terry Williams, raised five biological children and four adopted children in the Kirkwood community.

His children being refused service at a lunch counter spurred his involvement in the civil rights movement, where he became one of Martin Luther King, Jr.'s lieutenants. He was one of the organizers of the march in Selma, Alabama and was with King when he was killed. Back home, he organized the Feed the Hungry and Homeless campaign, which continues today. He served in the state House of Representatives from 1974 to 1985, as well as on the Atlanta City Council and DeKalb Board of Commissioners.

Williams was as colorful a spokesman for civil rights as his frequent choice of attire: a bright red shirt, denim overalls, and red sneakers.

Dairies and Farms

In 1920 that tiny invader, the boll weevil, forced DeKalb farmers to stop depending on cotton. While many gave up farming and moved to Atlanta to take up other occupations, others turned to diversified crops and dairy farming.

DeKalb had many farms, some producing enough crops to sell and others simply feeding their own families.

Agricultural methods developed by local farmers like Richard Sams had farm-

✧ *Richard F. Sams, Jr. applied principles he learned while earning a degree in chemical engineering from Georgia Tech to his 200-acre truck farm just off on Lawrenceville Highway. From the 1920s until he retired in 1959, he grew spinach, turnips, tomatoes, string beans, butter beans, collards, and raspberries. Known as the "number one vegetable man of the nation," he used innovative practices, such as soil replenishment, refrigeration, and irrigation. Some ninety acres of his farm was taken for the I-285/I-78 interchange. The interchange was named for Sams in 1992.*

ers all across the nation looking to DeKalb for leadership in modern techniques. DeKalb County was described as the "Pearl of the Piedmont."

Richard Sams, Sr. had been farming for many years before his son, Richard, Jr., bought 200 acres adjoining his father's property and started his own farm. A Georgia Tech graduate, Richard Jr. used advanced technologies, like soil sampling, refrigeration, and irrigation in the 1920s, before anyone else in the area. He rotated crops with soybeans to enrich the soil and started tomato plants in steam-heated greenhouses to have the earliest tomatoes. The farm produced collards, spinach, turnip greens, tomatoes, peaches, strawberries, corn, raspberries, mustard greens, and other vegetables, and sold them in Atlanta. In its heyday, the farm was one of DeKalb's largest employers. A newspaper of the day called Sams "the number one vegetable man in the nation."

The farm, once 350 acres, gradually was surrounded by development. In 1964 Richard Sams, Jr. sold 88 acres to the Georgia Department of Transportation for construction of the I-285 perimeter highway. In 1991, the Stone Mountain Freeway/I-285 interchange was named the Richard F. Sams Interchange.

Though farms were important, what truly rejuvenated DeKalb's economy was dairy farming. At one time, all the undeveloped land in DeKalb was zoned for dairies. DeKalb became the leading producer of dairy products in the Southeast. In the 1930s DeKalb had more dairies than any county outside the state of Wisconsin.

Among the best known dairy farms in DeKalb were Ross, Cox, Pierce, Hyde, and Irvindale.

One dairy was unique. Mathis Dairy on Rainbow Drive in south DeKalb not only was a certified dairy, it also it is well remembered by the thousands of children and families who visited the farm, its public picnic areas and, most of all, Rosebud, the county's most famous cow. Mathis was not just a dairy, it was a beloved a community institution.

Robert Lloyd Mathis came to DeKalb from Stewart County in 1917 at the age of 21. With a widowed mother and two young sisters to support, he purchased 100 acres of land in the Panthersville community. The land came with five cows and a Model T Ford. Just three years later, a local newspaper called Lloyd Mathis "one of the most successful young dairymen in DeKalb." Mathis named the road in front of his diary Rainbow Drive because he said he had built a pot of gold at its end.

He hired his first employee, Herman Parker, in 1918, and they worked together 50 years, through good times and bad. Both drove the delivery routes, but Parker kept all routes in his head. The number of employees grew, of course, and ultimately would include Mathis' entire family. Lloyd Mathis married Essie Cook, known as "Miss Cookie." Their children, Bob, Pat, Betty, and Jack, all worked in dairy. In the early days, Cookie prepared the noon meal for everyone.

Mathis was the first in the county to qualify as a certified dairy, in 1928, meeting all the standards that were much stricter than for production of Grade A milk. Mathis was the only DeKalb dairy allowed to sell certified raw milk. Cows and employees were chosen for their superior health and checked regularly by doctors. Milk was produced in a sterile environment, and their entire operation was supervised by the Fulton County Medical Society Milk Commission. Mathis cows were always fed a diet free of herbicides and pesticides.

Beyond the regulations, Lloyd Mathis was fanatical about cleanliness and freshness and careful about appearances. Cows got two baths a day, and even trucks were washed daily. Home delivery was guaranteed within 24 hours of milking. Scratched bottles were always discarded. Mathis himself wore a tie every day.

Many dairies went out of business during the Depression. Mathis Dairy allowed needy customers to get milk "on account." After the Depression, Lloyd Mathis destroyed the account book.

A chance happening moved Mathis Dairy beyond being just an outstanding dairy operation to being renowned. Boy Scouts needing qualifications for a badge occasionally visited the dairy. Herdsman J.

✧ *From 1920s to 1930s, much of north DeKalb looked like this pastoral view of the W.O. Pierce Dairy in Chamblee. During decades DeKalb County produced as much milk as any other county in the nation.*

J. Wade led the tours and once let a Scout milk a gentle cow, the only Gurnsey among a herd of Holsteins. Word got out, and every child wanted to milk a cow. When a newspaper reporter got wind of the story, he wanted to know the name of the cow. The story goes that Pat Mathis fielded the call. Pat's University of Georgia roommate, whose nickname was Rosebud, happened to enter the room, and spontaneously the cow's name became Rosebud. The roommate, Ben Miller, grew up to be a Georgia Superior Court judge and often repeated the story.

From then on, the dairy was geared to visitors, especially children. There were creative names for cow dormitories like Moo-Tel, and feeding areas were called Calf-a-Terias. Calves wore blankets that read, "My mother works for R. L. Mathis Dairy." There were coloring books, souvenir "I milked Rosebud" buttons, and free chocolate milk. The lake was a popular destination for field trips, picnics, and corporate outings. The dairy even added a petting zoo. The property averaged 300 visitors a day, six days a week, with more than a thousand on weekends. There was never a charge.

Rosebud was a star. She visited the governor's mansion, the state capitol, and the top of Stone Mountain. A scavenger hunt had participants looking for cream for their coffee. The winner found Rosebud on top of Hyatt Regency Hotel in downtown Atlanta. Every politician had to be photographed milking Rosebud. She even was featured on the *Candid Camera* television show, with bewildered city kids trying to milk the cow.

✧ *U.S. Senator Herman Talmadge is pictured milking Rosebud at Mathis Dairy. Milking Rosebud was one of the most sought-after political photo opportunities of the 1960s through the 1980s.*

JACK MATHIS.

The Mathis family became well known in DeKalb, active in church, civic, and philanthropic endeavors. Ironically, Lloyd Mathis, who quit school in the fifth grade, grew up to be an enthusiastic supporter of education. He was a trustee of the Little Red School, a forerunner of Southwest DeKalb High School.

DeKalb's last working dairy, Sheppard's Dairy on South Hairston Road, closed in 1995. The last working farm, where Silvey Vaughters raised dairy cows, beef cattle and hay, was sold to the state of Georgia in 2002. The farm is now part of the Arabia Mountain Heritage Area in southeast DeKalb, which was designated as a federal heritage area in 2006.

✧ *Silvey Brice Vaughters and Rebecca Cown married in 1937, and bought some rundown farm acreage on Klondike Road in 1946. Together they built the place into a respected farming operation, breeding prize-winning Jersey and Angus cattle, and raising, horses, chickens, ducks, and hogs. Vaughters, who also taught school, built the county cannery, and sold insurance, is known for his love of bluegrass music.*

CAROL VAUGHTERS SELLARS.

DeKalb Police Officers Lewell C. (Louie) Henderson and Miles Henry (Dock) Phillips were killed August 12, 1927. Their story would make a good ballad. The pair was riding in the county's brand new Lincoln police car and crashed while chasing moonshiners.

Dock and Louie

Bootlegging—illegal making, selling and distributing liquor—was big business in DeKalb in late 1920s. Stories from the period read like ballads: stalwart lawmen in fast cars chasing devious, evil law-breakers in even faster cars down dirt roads in the dead of night.

In 1927, determined to end the menace once and for all, DeKalb bought a Lincoln Touring Car, the most powerful vehicle on the road at the time. Taxpayers raised the roof about buying that car, also one of the most expensive cars of its day.

In the dark hours of early morning on August 12, Officers Dock Phillip and Louie Henderson were riding the bootlegger beat in the brand-new Lincoln. Louie was well known in north Georgia as a relentless pursuer of evildoers. He once disguised himself and worked alongside a murder suspect for a week before he could get the drop on him. Said one fellow officer: "This was a bad guy who said he wouldn't come back alive. But Louie didn't care. He was all man himself."

In the new Lincoln, Louie and Dock were speeding down Briarcliff Road in pursuit of a car loaded with illegal booze.

Officers Oscar Bell Rowell and Henry Smith were scheduled to meet Dock and Louie at Jones' Store at Briarcliff and Clairmont, but their fellow officers never showed, and the pair went looking for them. Rowell and Smith soon were caught up in a chase of their own down Clairmont and later North Decatur Road, hitting speeds of 85 miles per hour. The whiskey runners' "block car" dropped behind the three bootleggers' cars, and the occupants started throwing roofing tacks onto the road. Rowell and Smith's Buick blew a tire, and the bootleggers sped away into the night. Rowell and Bell were changing a flat tire on the side of the road when another officer came along to tell them about Dock and Louie.

The pair had wrecked, and Dock was killed. Louie was taken to Emory Hospital, but died before morning.

"Nobody ever knew what happened to Dock and Louie on Briarcliff Road. Some said bootleggers set up a road block trap for the Lincoln, and others said a smoke screen got them," Officer Rowell said many years later in an interview with DeKalb Police Chief Robert T. Burgess, who wrote the book, *History of DeKalb County Police 1914-1964*.

"They were two of our best officers, and the bootleggers referred to them as 'Dock and Louie in that damn fast Lincoln.'... Anyway, that ended the Lincoln and Dock and Louie and all the gripes about us having the Lincoln. It went straight to the scrap pile."

Druid Hills

In 1893, Atlanta developer Joel Hurt organized the Kirkwood Land Company and hired noted landscape designer Fredrick Law Olmsted to design "the ideal residential suburb" just to the east of downtown Atlanta in DeKalb County. He predicted that "the handsomest residences in the South will be located in Druid Hills."

Although Druid Hills is scarcely four miles from Centennial Olympic Park, it was considered the suburbs at the turn of the nineteenth century.

Already 71 years old, Olmsted had already completed Central Park in New York City. He also designed the grounds of U.S. Capitol and the Biltmore Estate in Asheville, N. C. Although he created the design of linear parks, Olmsted died 1903 before finishing Druid Hills. Olmsted Brothers, run by his sons, finished the construction, which began in 1905 and finished in 1936.

Hurt sold the development to a new company, owned by Coca-Cola magnate Asa Candler, Sr., in 1908 for "a cool half million," according to a front-page announcement in the *Atlanta Journal*. It was the largest land sale ever recorded in the southern states. The tract began at the intersection of Ponce de Leon and Moreland and ran parallel to and a mile north of the Georgia Railroad almost to Decatur, then north along Briarcliff Road for several miles. Preston S. Arkwright and Forrest and George Adair, William D. Thomson, Harold Hirsch, and John S. Candler (Asa's brother) also were shareholders in the new company called Druid Hills.

Olmsted's plan called for a curving, tree-lined boulevard with parks in the median, bordered by large estates. The intent was to provide a pleasant drive, allowing workers who had spent all day in the hot, dusty city to relax before arriving home. The result transformed a dirty, dangerous track called Green Street into Ponce de Leon Avenue, an 80-foot-wide boulevard that stretched from Briarcliff Road to the Decatur city limits.

✧ *Callanwolde, the Gothic-Tudor home of Charles Howard Candler, was abandoned, dilapidated, and frequented by vagrants in the early 1970s, when a grassroots campaign purchased it for DeKalb County. Today Callanwolde is the county's premiere arts center, hosting classes, exhibits, and performances.*

JOE LEE COLLECTION

By June of 1917, improvements to the new 1,492-acre subdivision included roads, sanitary services, water and gas lines, sidewalks, trees, golf club and clubhouse, and electric car line, all at a total cost of more than $800,000.

Well-known architects, such as Neel Reid and Philip Trammel Shutze, designed the houses. Prominent residents included Asa Candler and members of his extended family, Samuel Pattillo and his son John Ray Pattillo, owners of the Pattillo Lumber Company, and William D. Thompson, dean of the Emory University Law School, among others.

The first home to be built in Druid Hills was that of Judge John S. Candler. A brick dwelling on a modest four and one-half acres at the corner of Ponce de Leon Avenue and Briarcliff Road, it was completed in 1909. It was notable for its four bathrooms, one for every bedroom. Judge Candler died in 1941, and the home was torn down in 1952. Asa Candler did not move to the neighborhood until 1916, when he built his home on Ponce de Leon Avenue near Oakdale Road. The home, built for entertaining, was visited by President Howard Taft and famous evangelist Billy Sunday.

By comparison, the next generation of Candlers built far more elaborate estates.

Asa Candler, Jr. built on 42 acres on Briarcliff. His property included a golf course, two swimming pools, and a zoo which housed elephants (Coca, Cola, Refreshing, and Delicious), lions, baboons, a Bengal tiger, a black leopard, and a gorilla. Neighbors claimed they lived in fear of the animals. One neighbor sued and won $25,000 because she found a baboon sitting in the driver's seat of her car. The baboon snatched her purse, and in the struggle to retrieve it, the woman said she fell and broke her leg. The suit resulted in Candler's giving the animals to the city of Atlanta. Candler's animals formed the basis for the city's first zoo.

Charles Howard Candler, Asa's eldest son, was president of The Coca-Cola Company and chairman of the Board of Trustees of Emory University. He began construction in 1917 on a new house on 27 acres on Briarcliff Road. One of the leading architects of the day, Henry Hornbostel, who also designed Emory University, designed the Gothic-Tudor mansion in the style of an English country home. The name is a salute to the family's Irish ancestry. Callanwolde translates to "Candler forest." The original estate included a four-car garage with four-room apartment upstairs, greenhouse,

✧ *In 1893 Atlanta developer Joel Hurt said that Druid Hills would contain "the handsomest residences in the South." The only part of the dream to be realized under Hurt's leadership was the linear parks designed by Fredrick Law Olmsted. Hurt sold the Kirkwood Land Company to Asa Candler in 1908 for "a cool half million." Candler finished the development, which featured houses by Neel Reid, Philip Trammel Shutze, and other noted architects. Several Candler family members had handsome homes in Druid Hills.*

JOE LEE COLLECTION

✧ *Asa Griggs Candler built his house on Ponce de Leon Avenue in his new Druid Hills subdivision in 1916 for the sum of $210,000. His wife, Lucy Elizabeth Howard Candler, died three years later while the house was still only partially furnished and the landscaping incomplete. Candler continued to live there with his second wife until 1926, when he became ill. The house was later rented and then used as a boarding house until the Atlanta Melkite Community purchased it in 1957 for only $62,000. The former Coca-Cola magnate's home now is the St. John Chrysostom Melkite Catholic Church.*
JOE LEE COLLECTION

conservatory, and buildings for cows, horses, chickens, and turkeys. There were formal, informal, and vegetable gardens, as well as fruit and nut trees. The grounds also included a swimming pool with two-story Tudor clubhouse and tennis courts.

Two features were unique even to the lavish standards of Druid Hills. An Aeolian organ with 3,742 pipes in the Great Hall, powered by air from blowers in the basement, played music from paper rolls. A sound system, hidden behind carved tracery, allows the music to be heard throughout the house. In the basement is a single-lane bowling alley.

Callanwolde was home to the Candler family until two years after his death in 1957. After changing hands several times, the mansion survived years as an neglected property, including a fire set by vagrants in the early 1970s. A huge public fund-raising campaign, spearheaded by the Druid Hills Civic Association, secured it in 1972 for the county to use as its flagship arts center. The completely restored mansion now is maintained cooperatively by the Callanwolde Foundation and DeKalb County.

Callanwolde has been the scene of many weddings and gala events, as well as the filming of several movies. During the 1996 Olympics, the mansion served as headquarters for the Italian Olympic Committee.

Walter Candler, third son of Asa, Sr., built Lullwater Farms on 185 acres on Clifton Road. The property was enhanced by a 25-acre lake, tennis courts, swimming pool, stables, hunting lodge, and a half-mile horse race track. Candler sold Lullwater Farms to Emory University in 1958; the house is now home to Emory's president.

In all, Asa Candler and his relatives built ten mansions in Druid Hills. Of the four original Candler brothers, two lived in Druid Hills. Warren Candler lived nearby on North Decatur, and Milton lived in Decatur.

A 1986 magazine article pointed out that seven of the Candler houses were still standing, but only two were private residences and none were owned by the Candler family.

For years, Druid Hills was a self-contained enclave for DeKalb's richest families. Emory Village was built in 1924 to provide retail necessities. Privately-operated schools, fire, and police services—even a water system—all were available within the community.

The Druid Hills ideal is said to have served as inspiration for Avondale Estates and other Atlanta area neighborhoods.

One notorious tragedy has marred the community's peaceful existence over the years. On September 29, 1943, an intruder murdered C&S Bank executive Henry C. Heinz, husband of Asa Candler's only daughter, Lucy, in their Ponce de Leon Avenue home. Atlanta and DeKalb police and Lucy's son-in-law, Dr. Bryant K. Vann, responded to her calls for help. In

✧ *The Druid Hills Homeowners Association proved in 1985 that its members are not afraid to take on anyone—even a former president of the United States. The "Road Busters" chained themselves to trees and created a tent city in Fredrick Law Olmsted's linear park to protest the building of a road proposed to service President Jimmy Carter's presidential library. The road originally was intended to go through Druid Hills and Decatur and connect to the Stone Mountain Freeway. Protestors manned picket signs saying "Trees are Carter's hostages" and "Carter and Moreland [the state road commissioner] are highwaymen." The spectacle stopped traffic on Ponce de Leon Avenue and was called the best show in town. The protestors ultimately were successful, and only a small portion of the road, called Freedom Parkway, was ever built.*

the dark, both Vann and the police thought the other was the intruder. A gun battle ensued, leaving Vann and several officers wounded. The arrival of other relatives and neighbors, as well as the driver and passengers of a passing streetcar, added to the confusion.

Heinz was city chairman of the banking division of the third War Loan Drive, among his many civic endeavors. He stayed up past his bedtime to catch a radio news report on the drive, which had reached its goal. Had he gone to bed he might never have crossed paths with the burglar.

More than a year later, Horace Blalock was convicted of the crime. Blalock admitted to being the burglar who terrorized the Druid Hills neighborhood. He had burglarized the Heinz home three times.

Druid Hills Parks and Parkways were named to the National Register of Historic Places in 1975. The remainder of the Druid Hills Historic District was added in 1979.

Early Political Drama

The years immediately following the Civil War were politically among the most lively and infamous in the state's history. Several players on this tumultuous stage made their homes in DeKalb County. Robert A. Alston, John Brown Gordon, Alfred Holt Colquitt, Warren A. Candler, and Rebecca Latimer Felton all made their mark on the state

The abolition of slavery left Georgia with no cheap source of labor. At the same time, state government coffers were at an all-time low. Prisons were overflowing, largely with black inmates, and the government could not afford to keep them fed, housed, and clothed.

The convict lease system, begun in 1868, provided what the government believed was an innovative solution. Private individuals and corporations could pay the government for the use of convicts. The government not only did not have the expense of maintaining the convicts, leases also put extra dollars into the state's depleted coffers.

✧ *Robert Alston died on March 11, 1879 as a result of a duel with Edward Cox over the convict lease system. Alston and Cox are buried near each other in the Decatur Cemetery.*

Lessors were charged with providing adequate food, clothing, and shelter for prisoners, but abuses were universal. Convicts were housed in camps where they were chained, starved, and beaten. Female inmates were raped, both by overseers and by other prisoners. Many convicts died.

While many believed the convict lease system was simply a new form of slavery, some felt it was even worse. While slave owners had a vested financial interest in keeping slaves in good health, those who leased convicts had no such interest—either financial or moral. Because there was little or no overhead involved beyond paying the annual state fee, lessees stood to make substantial profits by using convict labor.

DeKalb County citizens were at the forefront of the acrimonious debate that raged on both sides of the issue. One gave his life in the effort to reform the state's prison system.

Robert A. Alston was born in Macon on December 31, 1832. A Confederate veteran, he settled with his family in DeKalb's East Lake community. His house, accepted onto the National Register of Historic Places in 2004, has been restored by the current residents.

Alston was a farmer, journalist and lawyer in 1878 when he was elected to the state House of Representatives. He was a staunch advocate of prison reform and campaigned for dissolution of the convict lease system. In 1879 he was asked by his friend, U.S. Senator John B. Gordon, to find a buyer for his leases. Edward Cox, who sub-leased 60 of Gordon's convicts, objected to Alston's handling of the matter.

Cox stalked and threatened Alston, who repeatedly tried to avoid the conflict. Alston finally purchased a gun for protection. At mid-afternoon on March 11, 1879, Cox caught up with Alston in the office of the treasurer in the state capitol. In the ensuing gun battle, each man was struck. After Alston had fired his last bullet, Cox shot Alston in his right temple. He died at the nearby residence of a physician.

Cox was convicted of murder and sentenced to life in prison, but was pardoned after serving only a short time… none of it as a leased convict. He died on his farm on Marietta Road in 1901 and is buried in the Decatur Cemetery, ironically a short distance from Robert Alston.

John B. Gordon, considered one of the best of the Confederate generals, moved to the Kirkwood section of DeKalb after the Civil War. Born in 1832, in Upson County, he was never very successful as a businessman or lawyer, but managed to turn his war fame into peacetime popularity with Georgia voters. A charismatic orator, he dabbled in publishing, insurance, and railroads.

He was elected to the U.S. Senate in 1872 and was the first Confederate to preside over that body. Gordon and his friends Alfred Holt Colquitt, another Confederate veteran and DeKalb citizen, and war era Governor Joseph E. Brown were called the Bourbon Triumvirate, leaders of the state Democratic party which supported a return of the antebellum power structure. They also worked

✧ *Born near Lithonia, Rebecca Latimer Felton was the first female U.S. senator. This photo was taken on the day she addressed the Senate, Nov. 22, 1922.*

to industrialize the state, including promoting railroads.

Gordon, Brown, and Colquitt, the three most powerful men in post-Reconstruction politics in Georgia politics, all spoke out against the convict lease system. As governor in 1886, Gordon vowed he would end it. However, they all also understood that the system provided enormous profits for the renters and that the state could not afford to care for the prisoners. Finally, in 1908, when the full extent of the inhumane conditions came to light, the state legislature outlawed the practice. Decatur resident and Warren Candler's nephew, Charles Murphey Candler, authored the landmark bill.

The Bourbon Triumvirate came under a great deal of criticism in 1880 when Gordon resigned his U.S. Senate seat to become the legal counsel for the Western and Atlantic Railroad. Brown, who was president of the railroad, was appointed by then-Governor Colquitt to fill Gordon's unexpired Senate term. Gordon quickly made a great deal of money. Eight years later Gordon became governor. Critics charged that the three had cut a deal.

Despite all the allegations and criticism, Gordon remained a popular figure. Three years after his death in 1904, the state erected a huge monument on the grounds of the state capitol, the general astride a horse, created by Solon Borglum, brother of the first Stone Mountain carver. Gordon is buried in Atlanta's famed Oakland Cemetery.

Gordon and Colquitt were the only two governors ever elected from DeKalb.

Georgia's feisty grand dame of politics, Rebecca Latimer Felton, did not share other Georgians' good opinion of Gordon. She was always convinced that he had something to do with her friend Alston's death. The belief may have stemmed from the bad feeling between the two, which began during a bitter political campaign. Gordon campaigned against William H. Felton, Rebecca's husband, when Felton ran in 1874 for the Seventh District seat in the U.S. House of Representatives as an Independent Democrat.

Born between Decatur and Lithonia in 1835, the daughter of progressive parents, Charles and Eleanor Swift Latimer, Felton received considerably more education than was considered proper for a female at that time. William Felton, a minister and physician, was several years her senior and the commencement speaker at her college graduation ceremonies. Rebecca climbed out of the second-story window of her parents' home to elope with Felton.

In a day when women were limited to tending their homes and raising children, Rebecca served as her husband's campaign manager and went with him to Washington as his secretary. She helped him write speeches and draft legislation. As the South's best known suffrage and prohibition campaigner, she ignored the mandate that women could not speak in public. Never one to back down from a fight, she took her campaigns to newspapers where her pen was feared by many in power.

By promoting their progressive reform agenda, William and Rebecca Felton made numerous enemies among the rich and powerful. Rebecca and Methodist Bishop Warren Akin Candler both supported prohibition, but they agreed on little else. The bishop, a member of the wealthy and influential Candler family, was so certain that the Women's Christian Temperance Union was secretly promoting women's right to vote that he successfully convinced his family members to cut off financial contributions for the WCTU. Rebecca also supported public education, particularly the University of Georgia. Candler, who was president and chancellor of Emory College, a Methodist institution, believed that only religious denominations were capable of operating appropriate institutions of higher learning.

With the passage of the Eighteenth (prohibition) and Nineteenth (women's suffrage) Amendments to the U.S. Constitution, Rebecca Latimer Felton saw two of her hard-fought campaigns bear fruit, both in 1920.

Rebecca's crowning personal moment came in 1922, at the age of 87, when Governor Thomas Hardwick appointed her to fill the unexpired term of U.S. Senator Thomas E. Watson. She only served for one day until a new senator was sworn in, but in her speech, she predicted that women in the Senate one day would not be a novelty. Felton died in 1930 in Cartersville, where she is buried.

While she lived her adult life in Bartow County, DeKalb claims her as one of its most famous women. Her accomplishments and contributions to Georgia were numerous, among them three books, one of which, *Country Life in Georgia in the Days of My Youth*, details her years in DeKalb County.

Public Safety

Law enforcement was one of the first items on the agenda when DeKalb County was organized. The Georgia legislature commissioned John S. Welch as the first sheriff on March 18, 1822. In order to be eligible to hold the office, Welch had to swear he had never been involved in a duel. As the county was only one year beyond being Indian territory, Welch was unprepared for its first prisoner. Allen Burch was convicted of involuntary manslaughter and ordered taken to the

Gwinnett County jail because there was no safe jail in DeKalb.

The county's first jail, located on McDonough Street just south of the courthouse square, was a small two-story log building, with the first floor being a dungeon-like cell in which the worst criminals were confined. The only access to the cell was through a trap door in the floor which, when open, revealed a stairway. Entrance to the top floor was by stairs on the outside of the building. This log jail continued in use for about twenty-five years, until a granite structure was built. The county paid James R. Evans $5,500 to build a second jail in 1849.

Decatur was a rough-and-tumble place in the 1820s, with more taverns than churches. A Decatur blacksmith, Nathan W. Wansley, had a piece of his nose bitten off in a fight in 1824. His assailant, whose name has been forgotten, was found guilty of "mayhem." On this occasion, the punishment was "standing in stocks." Although the wooden pillory was designed to expose the offender to public ridicule, Sheriff George Harris must have taken pity on him because he hung a blanket on the jailhouse porch so passersby could not see.

Harris was the first sheriff elected by the people of the county. He had his hands full just keeping up with complaints lodged by residents on both sides of the Chattahoochee River near Sandtown in the southwestern area of the county. Both Indians and whites lodged allegations of "pilfering" and harassment. Of particular concern was a group of young whites called the "Pony Boys," who crisscrossed the river to stay out of the clutches of both Indian and white authorities.

The first death penalty sentence in DeKalb was handed down in 1829 during the administration of Sheriff John Brown. A man named Crowder murdered his wife and three children and set fire to their house to conceal the crime. He then cut his own throat, but lived to stand trial. His hanging on November 15, 1830 drew a large crowd to Decatur. Crowder was one of only three men ever hanged in DeKalb.

Some of the early crimes were not quite so serious, but needed attention nonetheless. Sheriff John Jones had to deal with unauthorized use of the county courthouse in 1840. Miscreants apparently used the courthouse at night for dancing and "disorderly collections." Jones solved the problem with a simple door lock.

Although a marshal officially was in charge when Marthasville (later Atlanta) was incorporated in 1843, the town still looked to DeKalb Sheriff John W. Fowler for most of its law enforcement. Justices of the Peace were responsible for day-to-day patrolling of both Marthasville and Decatur, the county's only two incorporated areas at the time. The DeKalb Grand Jury in September of 1844 scolded the JPs, saying, "The Grand Jury feels that there is too much indifference concerning municipal regulation of the towns of Decatur and Marthasville."

With the coming of the railroad, Atlanta became a rough frontier town, especially compared to the older, more sedate city of Decatur. The first mayoral election in 1848 featured two candidates: Moses W. Formwalt, representing the Free and Rowdy Party, and Jonathan Norcross of the Moral Party. At the age of 28, Formwalt, a Tennessee native who manufactured stills for a living, was declared the winner.

Two years after leaving office, Formwalt took a job as deputy sheriff for DeKalb County. He was stabbed to death by a prisoner in 1852 and is buried in Atlanta's Oakland Cemetery. His gravesite was unmarked until 1916, when a monument was erected. Formwalt Street in Atlanta was named in his honor.

Two particularly infamous areas served as havens for Atlanta's criminal element. Fed-up citizens took the law into their own hands in 1850, raiding Murrell's Row and burning it to the ground. Atlantans later raided Snake Nation in similar fashion.

Under Formwalt's administration, Atlanta got its first jail. Similar in design to most of the era, it did little to deter criminals. Prisoners could dig out from under the log buildings, which were set without anchor directly on the ground or on a stone foundation. A group of prisoners or friends could overturn the small buildings or lift them off the foundations.

Jonathan Norcross, for whom the Gwinnett County town is named, got his turn to be Atlanta mayor in 1851. His

✧ *DeKalb's law enforcement memorial was installed on the grounds of the Old Courthouse in 1997. Conceived by Police Chief R. T. Burgess, the monument contains the names of thirty-five officers of DeKalb and municipal police officers, as well as Derwin Brown, DeKalb sheriff-elect, and sheriff's deputy Moses Formwalt. The most recent addition was Dennis Stepnowski, who was killed in 2006.*

✧ *DeKalb's first jail was a small log building with a dungeon-like room for prisoners. A trap door in the floor of the main floor was the only access to the cells. In 1992, giant cranes marked the site of construction of a four-building complex that today is the county's fourth jail. The newest jail, located at the intersection of Memorial Drive and Interstate 285, has 3,600 beds and was built at a cost of $100 million.*

biggest challenge was regaining control of the town, which was ruled by the Rowdies. During one particularly heated confrontation, the Rowdies stole the War of 1812 cannon from the grounds of the Decatur courthouse and positioned it in front of the mayor's Atlanta store. Although the cannon was fired, neither the mayor nor his store was harmed, and the cannon was returned to the courthouse grounds.

Allen E. Johnson, DeKalb sheriff in 1850, was on hand on a pivotal day in Norcross's crusade against the Atlanta toughs. Found guilty in the mayor's court, the accused drew a knife and tried to get to Norcross. Johnson hit the man with his large hickory cane. He, his deputy Ben Williford, and two other men subdued the prisoner. It was the beginning of the end for the toughs.

Shortly after the end of the Norcross term, on December 20, 1853, Fulton County was carved out of the western side of DeKalb. Although DeKalb County was half of its original size, crime was still a problem.

James Paden, foreman of the DeKalb Grand Jury, wrote in 1853, "We had hoped the time had arrived when the commission of crime would be less frequent, but we must say we are disappointed that, notwithstanding the strong arm of the law, has and is being enforced against all offenders, that crime still stalks abroad. The perpetrators of crime are like the plagues went upon Egypt. When one is removed from jail to be hanged or sent to the penitentiary, there is another ready to step in. Are these things to continue?" By 1856, the bad guys apparently had decided to move on, and the grand jury issued a more optimistic assessment.

The sheriff's department was the sole peace-keeping agency of the county until after the turn of the nineteenth century. Deputies were aided by volunteers who were constantly on stand-by to fight fires in every community.

It was not until 1913 that the Decatur City Council voted to purchase boots, helmets, and fire coats for the town's volunteer fire company. That same year, it passed a resolution to buy a fire bell to sound the alarm in case of fire. Anyone caught ringing the bell maliciously was to be punished for disorderly conduct. The following year, the city purchased its first fire truck for $8,000 from the American LaFrance Fire Engine Company. At that time, the council also hired its first two paid firemen—a chief and assistant chief.

The volunteers were exempt from paying the street tax as long as they served. Later they were paid $1 for each practice drill they attended. These were limited to one a month. As the city grew, the council hired a driver and assistant driver, who were paid $90 and $25 per month, respectively.

Decatur's company got its first real test on the morning of September 13, 1916, when fire broke out at the DeKalb County Courthouse. The Atlanta Fire Company came to Decatur to help fight the blaze.

In 1923, Fire Chief M. D. Googer was appointed the city's chief of police and sanitation, as well as the town marshal, at a salary of $2,400 per year. By 1931, the city had outgrown its volunteer fire department, and Chief C. W. Nunn recommended that it be abolished. The rules for the new paid firemen were strict. Only one member of the company, while off duty, could leave the city limits, and he had to report where he was going and when he would return.

About the same time the city of Decatur began to move from relying on volunteers to fight fires to a paid fire department, the county was organizing its first police department.

The Georgia legislature authorized the county to begin policing in 1914, some time after the cities of Lithonia, Clarkston, Chamblee, Stone Mountain, Kirkwood, Edgewood, and Decatur had departments. A. S. Robinson was the first chief in DeKalb. Millard D. Nash was the first county police officer, hired in 1915 to patrol the Tucker area. A second officer, J. W. Beauchamp, joined the force in 1916 to handle crowds and welcome visitors at Stone Mountain.

The early history of the DeKalb Police Department was compiled by retired

Police Chief Robert T. "Bobby" Burgess. Burgess reviewed old records and interviewed dozens of DeKalb countians. The most colorful stories came from Oscar Bell Rowell, who moved to DeKalb in 1911 from North Carolina at the age of 19. He became a DeKalb police officer in 1925, according to the old commissioner's minute books.

At the age of 72, Rowell accurately remembered the names of many of the law enforcement and county officials from his early days on the force: County Commissioner L. T. Y. Nash, Sheriff "Gus" McCurdy, jailer Jack Hall, solicitor Claude "Major" Smith, Clerk of the Court Ben F. Burgess, and Ordinary Judge George. He also knew the names of the chiefs for many years after he left the department.

Mr. Rowell recalled, "When I started to work for DeKalb County as a regular police officer, my salary was $125 per month. We often got a warrant for our pay check and had to discount them some at the bank in order to get them cashed. The county was broke at the time.

"A policeman's house was just as busy as the country doctor's house. Everybody had troubles, and theirs was the problem that would not wait until you were on duty. People worried you to death at home with silly things that didn't mean nothing."

It wasn't all cops and robbers, Rowell said. "The police did everything. We would carry children's groups to Grant's Park for the commissioner. We would ride the grand jury about the county and carry baskets to poor people. We watched the roads and sometimes helped fix bad spots right then. We ran escaped prisoners with bloodhounds and put down trouble at the chain gang camp."

John Wesley Webb and Sam Gentry were the first two officers killed in the line of duty; both were shot.

Webb and his partner, Robert House, stopped R. R. Black on March 16, 1919, on suspicion that he had stolen goods in his car. Black meekly allowed his car to be searched, but then shot both officers. Black fled to Detroit, but was later captured, tried, convicted, and sentenced to life in prison.

"Gentry chased a load of whiskey from Avondale up toward Decatur, and a man jumped off the load and ran behind some sign boards at Sams' Crossing on East College Avenue. Gentry chased the man behind the sign boards, and the man shot and killed Gentry. This was right at the Decatur city limits, between Avondale and Decatur, known as No Man's Land back then."

The department had no radios during the time Rowell was on the force. "In fact, there were very few telephones. Most of the roads were dirt, and we got our calls by sending out to find us, if it was real important. We hung around the court house, but the jail was our main control point. On the night duty and weekends, all calls were received at the jail.

Rowell's worst experience on the force was "that shooting scrape" with burglars in Brookhaven. Since his partner had gone home for the night, Rowell set out for the store being robbed on foot, stopping by the home of the postmaster, James Woodall, to enlist his aid. Rowell went in the front door, while Woodall covered the rear.

"Anyway, I walked right into a pistol being held by one of the burglars named Boyce, and he snapped it right in my chest several times, and the thing never did fire. The Lord was with me. I pulled the trigger on my gun and shot Boyce point blank. The other subject began to fire at me, and several bullets went right over my head, and I fired back and ran him into the bathroom, and he closed the door. When I forced him out of the bathroom, Boyce had run a few feet and fell dead in front of the soda fountain. I caught the other one waiting in a getaway car outside. The people had begun to gather from hearing all the gun fire and so I called Sheriff McCurdy on the phone and told him what had happened. He asked me if I needed any help, and I told him to send a hearse because I had just killed a man. I knew Boyce was dead. I told Sheriff McCurdy that I would get Woodall to help me bring the other two to the jail.

"I went back home and got the car, and I don't know how to express how I felt. I told mama that I had just killed a man, and I felt bad all inside. The newspaper people were bothering me more than anything else. Me and Woodall started out in the old Buick, and the road was mud and was very slick. We ran into a ditch and with the help of about two mules and some chains and about two and one-half hours of time finally got to the jail with the prisoners."

The DeKalb Fire Department began as the Druid Hills Fire Department on July 31, 1934. A private-subscription company, serving only the Druid Hills neighborhood, the department depended on *Old Maude*, a 1934 Federal fire engine, purchased by J. V. Draughn, owner of the company. *Old Maude* was sold to the city of Oxford Fire Department in Newton County in 1954.

DeKalb County purchased the department from Draughn in 1937 and began expanding service from the original "Old No. 1" station on North Decatur Road to all parts of the county. Population in the county grew rapidly beginning in the late 1940s. By the early 1950s the DeKalb Fire Department had twelve fire engines and more than seventy employees.

The department faced its greatest challenge in the spring of 1972, at the petroleum storage facility in the city of Doraville. In the predawn hours of April 6, gasoline fumes from an overfilled hauling truck flowed into an adjacent residential neighborhood, and came in contact with a furnace pilot light. The explosion completely consumed the home and sent flames shooting back to the massive storage tanks. The resulting fire burned for four days at the "tank farm." Fire fighters from around the country traveled to Doraville to assist in fighting the huge blaze.

DeKalb County later added emergency medical technicians to the fire department staff. A separate Emergency Medical Services department followed. All county police, fire and EMS departments currently operate under the Public Safety Department.

✧ *Decatur's first St. Patrick's day parade leader Maury Mable marched from 1895 to 1945.*

✧ *Mike Lynch followed Maury Mable as the leader of Decatur's St. Patrick's Day parade.*

St. Patrick's Day

Back in the days when streets ran on all four sides of Decatur's Square, a young man by the name of Maury Mable and two of his friends began a town tradition that lasted 70 years.

Decatur's unique St. Patrick's Day parade began in 1895 with three men declaring their love of their ancestral home. It quickly grew into a slightly larger parade, with the Decatur High School band, ROTC members, and 60 "lasses" from the St. Thomas More Catholic Church. A few years after the parade's inception Mable's two friends died. Mable, then the county surveyor, dapper in his vested suit, top hat, and spats, led the parade for fifty years until 1945. He died a year later.

News of the parade spread all the way to the Old Sod, where Mike Lynch read about it in a County Leitrim newspaper. He never dreamed he one day would emigrate to America, become DeKalb's fire chief, and succeed Maury Mable as leader of the St. Patrick's Day parade. Lynch, with his jaunty bow tie and top hat, led the parade from 1946 to 1953.

Lynch's grandsons, Jimmy and Joe Herberman, carried on the tradition into the 1960s.

✧ *Maury Mable led the St. Patrick's Day parade in 1945. In the background are the Woolworth store, Western Auto, and the DeKalb Theater showing* Weekend at the Waldorf *starring Lana Turner.*

Stone Mountain

Stone Mountain is today what it has always been—a landmark, a curiosity, and a place for contemplation and recreation.

Legends and family histories recount that the mountain's first owners thought the big rock was useless.

John W. Beauchamp's descendants tell the story that their ancestor gave Indians $40, a horse and some whiskey for the mountain. Beauchamp apparently thought it was worth more than a man who is said to have walked 60 miles only to find that his newly-acquired land "wouldn't grow beans." He traded the mountain for a mule to ride back home. E. V. Sanford is said to have traded the mountain for a rifle with which he could hunt his dinner.

While the mountain may not have been as valuable as bottom land along the South River for making a living, it still attracted many families who brought their picnic lunches and young couples who thought it a romantic destination. The first person to capitalize on the mountain's popularity as a tourist destination was Andrew Johnson, who built a hotel at the base of the mountain. The hotel was the first building in the village of New Gibraltar, which later became the town of Stone Mountain. Aaron Cloud built a 165-foot wooden tower on top of the mountain, which visitors could climb to get what must have been a remarkable view of the surrounding countryside. Not secured in any way, Cloud's Tower was swept off the mountaintop during a thunderstorm.

Efforts to quarry the mountain's abundant granite also began in the 1830s, but moving the stone to market was impractical until the coming of the railroad in the late 1840s. The granite industry drew stonecutters from England, Scotland, Wales, Sweden, Norway, and Italy. The rough newcomers to the Stone Mountain-Lithonia area were said to be so rowdy that Lithonia made Dodge City look like a "Sunday School picnic." Stone Mountain granite, mined mostly in the Lithonia area, has produced miles of paving blocks and curbstone, as well as more exotic uses like the steps of the east wing of the United States capitol and locks of the Panama Canal. As owners of Stone Mountain, brothers William and Samuel Venable controlled a good bit of the granite business in DeKalb, although families like the Davidsons were important in the industry. Samuel Venable was heavily involved in creation of the Confederate memorial on Stone Mountain.

The idea to use Stone Mountain had arisen periodically since Francis Tichnor suggested it in an 1869 poem. It gained steam after William H. Terrell wrote an editorial in *The Atlanta Constitution* in May of 1914, and John Temple Graves wrote another in June, 1914, in *The New York American*.

✧ *Dignitaries celebrated the unveiling of the Borglum's head of Gen. Robert E. Lee in 1924 by having lunch on the carving. Lee's shoulder was large enough to accommodate the luncheon party.*

JOE LEE COLLECTION.

✧ *Sculptor Augustus Lukeman (hand on sculpture) inspects the head of Robert E. Lee in this 1928 photograph. Lukeman, who began work on the carving in 1926, was the second sculptor to work on the project. His design formed the basis of the sculpture completed in 1970. Gutzon Borglum began work on the mountain in 1923, but left in 1925. Lee, the central figure, is as tall as an 8-story building.*

✧ *Augustus Lukeman's vision for the Confederate memorial carving takes shape below the original head of General Robert E. Lee designed by Gutson Borglum in this photo taken on June 7, 1928. Borglum's work eventually was blasted off the mountain. Lukeman's idea was to leave the legs of the horses unfinished to give the impression that the Confederate leaders were riding through clouds.*

SPECIAL COLLECTIONS DEPARTMENT, GEORGIA STATE UNIVERSITY LIBRARY

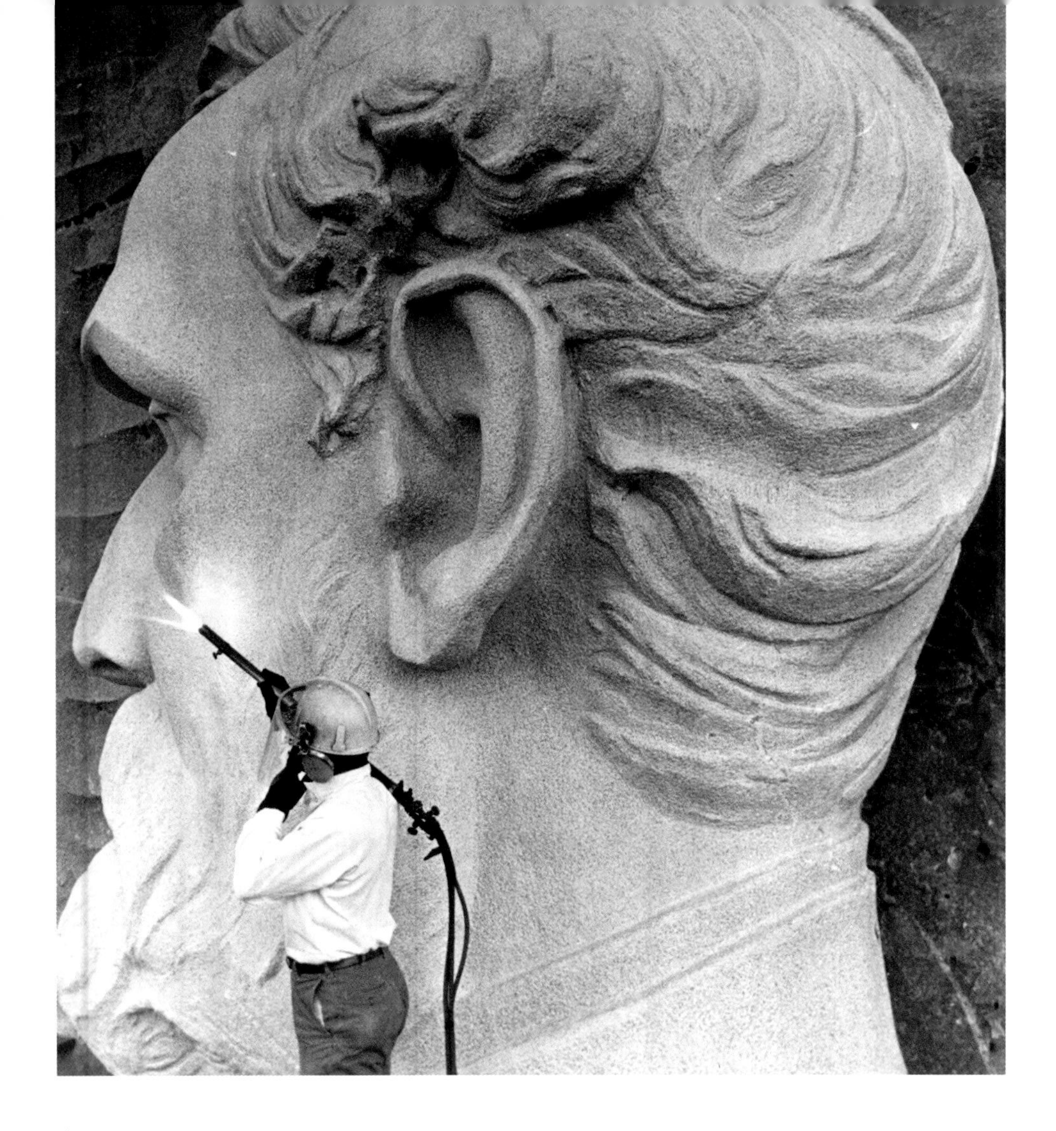

The sixteen-foot-high head of Gen. Robert E. Lee dwarfs the figure of chief carver Roy Faulkner as he applies finishing touches to Stone Mountain Memorial Carving. The entire figure of Lee is the height of an eight-story building. Faulkner, the memorial's final carver, is pictured here in about 1970.

But it took the passion and dedication of Helen Jemison Plane, an 85-year-old Confederate widow, to get the ball rolling. Mrs. Plane was one of the organizers of the Atlanta and Georgia chapters of the United Daughters of the Confederacy and went to the UDC for support for the idea. In 1914 the Atlanta Chapter of the UDC voted $100 to implement Mrs. Plane's idea of a 75-foot bust of Confederate Gen. Robert E. Lee on the north face of the mountain. Little did they know that it would be millions of dollars and fifty-six years later before Mrs. Plane's dream would become a reality.

Sam Venable owned Stone Mountain in 1914 and also was involved in the resurgence of the Ku Klux Klan, which had been dormant since 1869. In the fall of 1915, led by William J. Simmons, the Klan held its first cross-burning atop the mountain. Venable granted the Klan an easement to the mountain top in 1923; the easement was cancelled when the state purchased the property in 1958.

Ann E. Lewis remembers when she was Agnes Scott College student in 1920. "I vividly recall watching one night from a window on third floor Main, a mile or more parade of Ku Klux Klanners in white robes marching with torches on their way, I was told, to a midnight meeting atop Stone Mountain."

Also in 1915, Helen Plane and the UDC's new Stone Mountain Memorial Association committee hired sculptor Gutzon Borglum, whose plan was to carve into the face of the mountain the likenesses of Generals Robert E. Lee and Thomas J. "Stonewall" Jackson and Confederate President Jefferson Davis, surrounded by an astounding 700 to 1,000 other figures. In addition, Borglum wanted to carve an elaborate Memorial Hall into the base of the mountain.

The Venable brothers granted a 12-year lease for the portion of the mountain needed for the carving, and Borglum began work quickly. Materials were hauled up the mountain, and stairways were built to reach the carving location. A system of scaffolding and ropes was used to access the carving site on the sheer north face. Borglum developed a giant projector to throw images onto the mountain, and workmen painted the outlines of the figures.

But, lack of funding and World War I interrupted the work, and Lee's head was not finished until 1924. Dignitaries had lunch on Lee's shoulder as part of the unveiling festivities.

Also in 1924, the U.S. Treasury minted a commemorative fifty-cent coin that sold for one dollar in an effort to raise funds for the carving.

Friction between Borglum and the association, exacerbated by the ongoing funding problems, came to a head in 1925, when the association cancelled the sculptor's contract. In a fit of pique, Borglum destroyed his models. The association swore out a warrant for Borglum's arrest, but he fled to North Carolina, and the state refused to extradite him back to Georgia.

The association hired Augustus Lukeman in 1925, one week before Helen Plane died at the age of 96. The plan for the memorial was reduced to the central group of figures (Lee, Davis and Jackson), plus two color bearers and four other generals.

Jesse Tucker, who had been Borglum's superintendent of carving, was replaced by George Weiblen, whose family owned a stone company in Stone Mountain, and Italian sculptor Theodore Bottinelli, who worked for the Weiblens. Borglum's head of Lee was blasted off the mountain.

In November, 1927, the project suffered its first fatality: Thomas Kennedy, age 27, who fell from the scaffolding. The same year Elias Nour, who would become the famed "Old Man of the Mountain," rescued his first climber. The son of Lebanese immigrants who owned a diner at the base of the mountain, Nour rescued

36 people and six dogs between 1927 and 1963. He was awarded the Carnegie Medal of Heroism in 1953.

Funding for the memorial continued to be a problem, and relations between Sam Venable (a Borglum supporter) and the association deteriorated to the point that Venable refused to renew the lease and demanded an accounting of funds spent. Audits revealed that only 27 cents of every dollar raised were actually spent on the carving. The association was so badly in debt in 1929 that office furniture was sold to satisfy creditors.

Work stopped and for the next 30 years, various entities, both public and private, tried to resurrect the project, but financial problems and political squabbles always got in the way. In the meantime, Borglum, who tried in vain to get his job back, completed the sculptures at Mount Rushmore and died suddenly in 1941.

DeKalb Commissioner Scott Candler, a friend of the Venable family, is credited with the original plan to develop the mountain and surrounding acreage into a public park. In anticipation of fulfilling Candler's idea, the state created an authority to construct and manage state parks. A new sculptor—Julian Harris of Carroll County—was hired, and it appeared that the memorial would be completed at last. However, another war interrupted the process, and Harris never worked on the project at all.

Efforts were renewed in 1958, with an emphasis on developing the park, and five million dollars in bonds. DeKalb state Rep. James A. Mackay, as well as Stone Mountain attorney Douglas McCurdy, then state Secretary of Commerce Scott Candler, and Atlanta banker Mills B. Lane spearheaded the effort. Between 1958 and 1960 the state bought 3,200 acres surrounding the mountain for almost two million dollars.

Bill Thibadeau, chairman of the DeKalb Chamber of Commerce, wanted a "welcome house" at the mountain—one with indoor plumbing. At the time the only sign of life at the mountain was a little log house called The Studio, where two ladies sold gifts, and a path to two privies. Agnes Scott graduate and magazine publisher Ann E. Lewis chaired the Chamber's Tourist Committee, which raised $8,000 for materials. Prison labor was used to construct the facility. The two ladies moved their gift shop into the front room.

The idea of a reconstructed antebellum plantation soon followed. Scouts went all over Georgia to find right buildings. They did not have to look far for one of the buildings that represents a slave cabin. The cabin where Dr. Chapmon Powell and his wife raised their family was moved from Clairmont Road and currently resides in the complex. According to Lewis, "The mansion came from the Dickey community near Edison, having been sawed into four sections and trucked here... The house across the way from the 'big house' came from Kingston."

In 1962 the new Stone Mountain Memorial Association issued invitations to nine sculptors to submit proposals. The ideas ranged from the mundane to the bizarre; only one sculptor used the face of the mountain as a canvas. Public outcry was so intense that the association decided to finish the sculpture on the mountain. Although his proposal had been for a statue of a man holding a broken sword, Walker Hancock was hired to finish Lukeman's work.

The design was reduced to just the three figures, and Lukeman decided not to completely carve the horses' legs, but to have it appear as if the figures were galloping out of clouds. Hancock also made several improvements and corrections to Lukeman's original design.

George Weiblen returned as superintendent of carving, and Cohen "Dick" Ludwig was hired as head carver despite a fear of heights. Ludwig quit three times during his stint, but is credited with rescuing the head of Jackson after previous work was deemed unsatisfactory.

Modern work on the carving was made much easier by two innovations. The world's tallest outdoor elevator delivered workers and materials to the site much faster than the hundreds of steps previously used. A new thermo-jet torch, a vast improvement over the chisels and hammers originally used, made carving easier and faster. Much of the torch work was done by Roy Faulkner, who later became chief carver.

New tools and methods did not make the work less dangerous. Howard "Bollweevil" Williams fell some 400 feet to his death in 1966. All the workers except George Weiblen and Roy Faulker quit and had to be replaced. One of the replacements was Nelson Wilborn. Wilborn would die in a fall in 1971 as scaffolding was being removed from the face of the carving.

More than one hundred years after Francis Tichnor wrote his poem, the carving was finally finished in the spring of 1970. A second lunch on Lee's shoulder was held on a cold, blustery day in March. The official dedication was held on May 9, with Vice President Spiro Agnew as the keynote speaker. Reporters from around the world covered the event.

The international spotlight next shone on the Stone Mountain in 1996 when the park hosted the archery, tennis, and cycling events for the Olympic Games.

During the last 40 years, the park has developed into one of the most popular tourist attractions in the nation. Hundreds of thousands of tourists attend annual festivals and concerts, as well as the laser light show and the Easter sunrise service atop the mountain. New attractions, such as the 1870s replica of a Southern town called Crossroads, continue to be added to complement old favorites like the cable cars, riverboat, and carillon.

Energetic tourists and locals alike continuously use the county's oldest Indian trail, the 1.3 mile path that meanders up the gentle side of the mountain. Once atop the mountain, 1,683 feet above sea level, they are rewarded with grand views of downtown Atlanta and the north Georgia mountains.

INDEX

✧

This aerial shot of the Decatur Square shows the progress of the underground with MARTA rail station in about 1977 from high above Church Street (in the foreground). The current courthouse is the tall building on the left. The Old Courthouse is on the right. The Atlanta skyline can be seen in the background. Many residents were concerned about the safety of Decatur when the huge hole was dug to accommodate the underground commuter rail station. A portion of Sycamore Street was replaced by the station.

SHARING THE HERITAGE

Historic profiles of businesses, organizations, and families that have contributed to the development and economic base of DeKalb County

Special Thanks to

H&A International Jewelry, Ltd.

AMERICAN HERMETICS

It all started in 1974 when Paul Sykes unknowingly laid the foundation of a legacy, a legacy that would endure joy and hardship; a legacy that would be perpetuated by a company called American Hermetics.

The first block was laid in southern Florida where Paul began a small compressor remanufacturing shop. It was a two-man operation back then, but Paul knew that through perseverance, good customer service, and technical know-how that the field technicians could rely on, the company could survive and prosper, and it did. A wounded Vietnam War veteran, Paul was a mechanical engineer who had actually begun his career as a sales engineer for one of the nation's largest compressor firms, and while performing in this capacity he quickly surmised that he could do it better. It was this "can-do" attitude that led his company, American Hermetics to the position of being an industry leader. Over the next several years, Paul expanded the company into Georgia, Texas, and Louisiana. Meanwhile, on the personal side of his life, he married Bonnie, who not only provided him with a new family but would also take the position of Chief Financial Officer, enabling them to work hand-in-hand as they further grew the business. Eventually, leaving the south Florida shop in Miami operational, Paul moved his family into the Georgia area and took the helm in Decatur, leading American Hermetics through another round of expansion. This time the shops in Texas grew to four locations, and new shops were opened in Tennessee, North Carolina, and South Carolina. Today, American Hermetics has eleven locations spread across eight states and enjoys the reputation of being the most trusted in their industry.

Above: This artistic portrait of Paul Sykes pays tribute to the late founder in the foyer of the company headquarters.

Below: Paul and Bonnie Sykes with daughters, Jennifer Goodman (middle) and (back row, left to right) Julie Mikels, and Toni McElroy.

While operating in Decatur, the ideology that made American Hermetics prosper at its inception in Florida was the same good customer service and good product. What made these two aspects of American Hermetics exceptional were Paul's charismatic persona and his penchant for perfection. Every compressor is completely remanufactured. That means that every part of the compressor is either refurbished to meet OEM specifications or replaced with new parts. As an added feature, unique to American Hermetics, every compressor is operationally tested on a variable load R-22 test chiller. As far as the environmental conditions that the compressors are assembled in, one of Paul's favorite sayings was, "I can go broke clean as easily as I can dirty, so let's be clean." The fact is, that product quality is directly related to cleanliness, so "being clean" was not something that was just mentioned, it was a standard operating procedure, and has been for thirty-three years. The customer service was boosted by the fact that Paul believed in training his employees to know every aspect of how a compressor worked, and how they were assembled. "I believe in training even though it's expensive," Paul once remarked. "I want everyone in this building to be able to answer questions about our product." Paul even had his daughters remanufacture a compressor one evening after hours. "Since they were employees as well, they had to know what they were working with."

Paul's daughters, Julie, Jennifer, and Toni basically grew up in the shop. Julie remarks, "I always heard to never go into business with family. But at the same time we took great pride in how well family worked in our business. We have brothers, cousins, uncles, daughters, sons, sons-in-law, sisters, mothers, fathers, etc. Even in the toughest of times, American Hermetics managed to forge ahead. I often wonder if our success is contributed to, in part, by our involvement of family in all facets of our business." She also mentions that American Hermetics is not only her family business, but it is a family business for the employees as well, since most American Hermetics' employees are related to each other. "I take pride in how well our family works in business, as well as pats the back of all the employees we have working side-by-side with their kin." When asked how it was working for her father she said, "It was tough. He expected us to do no wrong, never be late, ever. But it was great. I loved growing up watching him work. I was always mesmerized by how well he treated and handled our customers. He was always so sure of himself. I loved that in him." She also says that in addition to watching her father she witnessed the influence of her mother. "I also had the opportunity to work closely with my mother. She always amazed me at how she could visualize the financial side of the company. She worked so hard, and watching them work that hard gave me a great appreciation of dedication and commitment."

Jennifer remembers her dad as a kind person who made things happen—a generous person who gave more than he had, or thought he would receive. "A lot of people didn't know that of him because he didn't advertise that about himself, but he worked with family, gave jobs to friends. He would loan them money, and he opened his home to them. You won't find a more generous person." She is also immensely proud of her father for the bravery he displayed at two of the most tumultuous points in his life; when he served in the United States Army in Vietnam as a consultant to the Vietnamese Army and when he battled cancer. "He was a true hero." As far as working with her dad, Jennifer remarks, "We daughters saw what it really takes to run a successful business. Work, work, a little fun, and more work, and not necessarily in that order." When you ask about the relationship of being an employee of her father, Jennifer said, "The summer after I turned fourteen all three of us daughters 'worked' for three weeks sorting parts. The

Above: The company exceeds industry standards by ensuring each compressor is tested in this variable load test chiller.

Below: American Hermetics' thirty-two-thousand-square-foot headquarters on Ponce de Leon Avenue in Decatur.

Above: Jimmy Dubroca and owner, Paul Sykes, dismantle compressor.

Below: Paul Sykes and crew, left to right, Dan Yarborough, Bryan Surfare, James "Red" Moore, Jimmie Goodman and Bill Reynolds after giving final approval to the compressor.

parts were upstairs in the warehouse in an area that was extremely dirty and had no air conditioning. Every night we would come home exhausted, dirty, and sweaty; it was not much fun. But at the end of that first week when we got that paycheck, I was pretty thrilled. I was thrilled about the money, yes; however, I was more thrilled when we got compliments from Dad on how well we had worked, and how proud he was of us."

After Julie and Jennifer moved away, the youngest daughter, Toni, worked summers. "We were always taught that being the boss' daughter does not equal a free ride. If nothing else, it meant you had to work twice as hard to prove yourself." And she did. "I started at the bottom making minimum wage." Toni worked every summer at American Hermetics until her junior year of college when she signed up for a college work program at Walt Disney World. "I learned a lot about customer service working there. I knew what customer service entailed but never really dealt with customers until then." As a testament to Paul's theory of customer service, Toni remembers, "He was adamant about returning phone calls. He would always say, 'Make sure you call everyone back as soon as possible.' Voicemail was never an option in our office; he saw it as a way of screening calls and thought it to be impersonal." In addition, Toni remarked, "He would always say that there needs to be a communication flow within the office. Everyone needs to be on the same page, so follow up and make sure nothing gets missed." After college Toni worked as the parts manager at American Hermetics. "I was in charge of making sure the guys had what they needed and could find it." As to the relationship of working for Paul she said, "There were a few things imbedded into me. Don't be late. It didn't matter if you were late by one minute or one hour, it was the same to him. I was never a morning person, so this was often a sore spot between us. Cleanliness: this was a biggie with Dad; he did not like a messy office, nor did he like piles on the desk. That was another sore spot." Other than American Hermetics and Walt Disney World, Toni has held a position as a mortgage lender. It was that experience that brought her back to American Hermetics. "I realized that I never again wanted to be encouraged to sell something to someone that they didn't need or couldn't afford." Once back, Toni began relieving her mother of the duties of CFO.

Bonnie remarks, "If nothing else, the success of American Hermetics enabled us to provide a good education for our children." All three daughters graduated from college: Julie with a degree in business from the University of Tennessee; Jennifer with degrees in International Studies and Spanish from Emory University; and Toni from Auburn University with a degree in Finance.

Fate took a turn for the worse in 2003 when Paul was diagnosed with cancer. He already had in mind a successor, but his diagnosis sped the process, and he knew the time had come to pass the torch and allow someone else to take the helm. Tony Mikels, who is married to Julie, had taken control of the South Carolina branch in 2000 and had been growing the business there with success. Before becoming part of the team at American Hermetics, Tony had attended the University of Tennessee, graduating with degrees in Human Resources and Business. He also served four years in the Untied States Navy as an anti-submarine warfare specialist and rescue swimmer, served six years in the United States Army as a Blackhawk pilot with tours of duty in the Kuwaiti war and Somalia, and in the Bahamas in conjunction with the Drug Enforcement Agency and the Bahamian Drug Enforcement Unit as an illegal drug trafficking intercept pilot. Additionally, he served as the Army Aviation Liaison Officer to the U.S. embassy in Nassau. Upon Paul's diagnosis, Tony moved his family to Georgia and took the helm in Decatur as president.

Today, Tony and Julie have three children. Jennifer is married to one of Paul's head field technicians, James Goodman, with whom she has two children. Toni holds the position of CFO at American Hermetics.

Unfortunately, Paul lost his battle with cancer in 2005, and although his presence will be missed, his influence remains. American Hermetics still adheres to the original foundation of good business practices set some thirty-three years ago in a small two-man shop in the south of Florida, but embraces the thirty year tradition of being a fixture in the landscape of Decatur, Georgia. Today, Tony is president and Toni McElroy is CFO. They, along with long-time foreman Terry Richards, comprise the management team of American Hermetics. Yes, the torch may have been passed and is now being held high by the next generation, but it still burns strong, and for as long as it burns, American Hermetics will continue to be a proud part of this community.

✧

Top, Left: In the early years, Jimmie Goodman and Paul Sykes check 150 ton Westinghouse compressors atop the Riveria Hotel in New Orleans, Louisiana.

Above: Carrier compressors displayed after spring inventory inspection.

Below: New Management team; Toni McElroy, Tony Mikels and Terry Richards.

D. W. Tench Grading and Hauling

✧

Above: A young Doug Tench poses for the camera while hauling firewood on his goat-drawn wagon as younger brother, Hoyt Tench, and Uncle Ed's dog look on.

Below: Doug remembers living in this house in Cornelia, Georgia, with his parents and grandparents. The house, built in the early 1900s, is still standing and still owned by the Tench family.

There were clues from the very beginning—such as when, as a little boy of nine or so, Douglas Wilson Tench would hitch a couple of goats to his wagon to haul firewood and pay Sunday afternoon visits to his neighbors.

There were clues later in life as well—such as when he became a teenager and helped his dad plow fields on the family farm, first with a mule and later with a tractor; a magnificent piece of machinery that dazzled him at first sight.

As he grew up and entered the service and then the workforce, pieces of the puzzle just kept falling into place until finally there was no denying what he was supposed to be doing.

Doug Tench was obviously fated to own a business and that business was to have something to do with tractors and a host of other dirt-moving, site-clearing, debris-hauling equipment. So, in 1960, armed with one small tractor and one big dream, he started that business in Doraville, Georgia.

Today, D. W. Tench Grading and Hauling has twelve full-time employees and a multitude of part-time laborers. The company also has a full fleet of dump trucks, tractors, front end loaders, track hoes, back hoes and almost every other piece of grading and hauling equipment imaginable, all of which Tench and his crew use six to seven days a week from sunup to sundown just to keep up with their ever-growing workload.

But, no matter how busy it gets, Tench says he would not dream of doing anything else.

"I like what I do so much that I don't feel right calling it work," the now seventy-six years-young Tench says. "Even when I'm on the job site before the rooster crows and after the sun goes down, I truly enjoy it."

While it is often said that a foundation is the most important part of a building, it is just as critical that a building site be properly prepared and graded before the foundation is laid. That is where Tench and his crew come in.

"We come in and push down trees, clear the site of all brush and haul all the stumps, limbs and debris to the landfill," Tench said. "We then level the ground for the foundation and, if required, we dig out the basement and come back to backfill once the foundation is laid. We also grade the driveway so that it can be paved and get the yard ready for landscaping."

"If there is a building on the site we're clearing, we demolish it," Tench continued. "My wife and I are certified in asbestos inspection and removal as well. This comes in handy when a building contains asbestos materials that need to be removed before demolition."

Although his company works for some commercial entities, they mostly work with builders and developers who develop residential subdivisions throughout DeKalb County and the Atlanta area. A few of the many DeKalb subdivisions they have helped create include Hunt Cliff, Dunwoody North, and Huntley Hills, a neighborhood he liked so much that he bought a corner lot and helped build the home he and his wife still live in today.

On the north side of Fulton County, his company has worked on the prestigious neighborhoods of Country Club of the South; and, in Duluth, the vibrant community of St. Ives is on their list of satisfied customers. They also prepared the site of the Ronald McDonald House on Houston Mill Road, Atlanta's first and the world's fourth Ronald McDonald House.

Like all of his customers, well-known Brookhaven builder Mac Byce has only great things to say about Tench and company.

"Tench Grading is the beginning of all my houses. Doug handles every opportunity as if he is trying to impress a new customer. There is not a better grading contractor in Atlanta," Byce said. "His combination of skill and ethics makes him the best. I consider Doug and his wife Mary family and would never think of using anyone else. He has completed all our houses which can be seen at www.bycehomes.com."

Aside from the usual yellow page listings, Tench says he has never found it necessary to place fancy advertisements or to delve into the world of high technology and websites. Most of his company's work comes through good old-fashioned word-of-mouth and the referrals of satisfied customers such as Byce and the many others he has worked with for decades.

"I have worked with some of these guys for 20, 25, 35 years even," Tench said proudly. "And, they continue to keep us busy with jobs and referrals."

✧

Above: Doug with one of his many trachoes at a jobsite in Midtown Atlanta.

Below: Doug grew up with four brothers. Here he poses with Hoyt (left) and Dewey (right). His other brothers are Donald and Dan, the latter who died at just 17.

It has really been that way from the beginning, added Mary, Tench's loving wife of forty years and the company's office manager and bookkeeper.

"Doug has never been afraid of hard work," she said. "I think he was born working and still hasn't slowed down. That's what makes him so successful and makes me so proud."

A native of Habersham County, Tench and his four brothers and three sisters were born into the farming family of Hezekiah and Viola Tench. From the time he was old enough to walk, he was proud to work alongside his father and mother in the fields and, by age thirteen, was plowing the farm's rich soils with help from the family mules, Bill and Sam. While he says he never minded plowing behind Bill or Sam, he admits it was really challenging sometimes, especially when the ground was hard from a cold, dry winter.

"I was so excited when we got our first tractor in 1947, my dad could hardly get me off of it," Tench reminisced. "I'd plow all day long. I loved that tractor. Come to think of it, I think that tractor is what started my fondness for all kinds of heavy equipment."

Though he loved life on the farm, Tench left home at age eighteen to begin finding his own way. He first landed in Michigan where he worked at an automobile manufacturing plant. He also spent some time driving a lumber truck before being drafted into the military. From 1951-1953, Tench proudly served as a United States Marine and was chosen to go to school to earn a Marine Core driver's license, a license that would allow him to drive all types of Marine vehicles and equipment. He finished at the top of his class, earning the highest scores on both the written and driving portions of the test.

"I did several things with that license, including driving the tankers that refueled planes. But, I have to admit it came in most handy when I was transferred to a new base. Everyone had to pull mess duty once a month—not the most popular job on base. However, when they saw I had a Marine license, they had me hauling groceries from the warehouse to the mess hall, and I never had to peel the first potato," Tench chuckled.

After finishing his tour with the Marines, Tench returned to Georgia and began working at the General Motors plant in Doraville. Though he says he enjoyed his job there, he could never quite get used to the hours.

"I worked an evening shift that started at 4:30 p.m. and, while I didn't mind working at night, I didn't know what to do with myself during the day," Tench recalled. "I was used to working from the time I woke up in the morning."

Tench said he began trying out some different things, but nothing really clicked until he ran across a small used tractor for

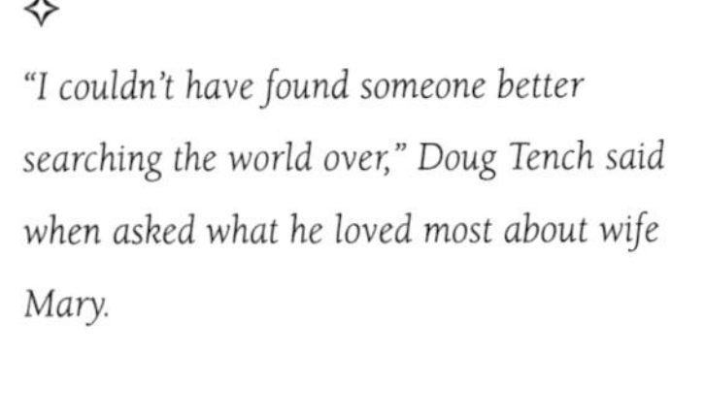

"I couldn't have found someone better searching the world over," Doug Tench said when asked what he loved most about wife Mary.

sale. He bought the tractor and was soon doing odd jobs such as plowing up the yards of new homes for landscaping.

"I remember it well. I think I made about $5 an hour for that first job," Tench said. He was soon not only preparing yards for landscaping, but he was doing the landscaping as well. In fact, it was not long before he had to buy another tractor; this one a little bit bigger.

"My customer base was growing. My phone was ringing consistently as my current customers kept referring me to new customers. I remember one time when a single customer referred me to seven others," Tench said. "Then, a salesman saw me and told me I needed a bigger tractor. Soon after I bought my largest yet—a Case front-end loader. I eventually decided to give up my General Motors job and hired my first full-time employee."

As his business continues to grow, Tench's equipment inventory also grows. And, when he buys a newer, bigger piece of equipment, he still lights up like a child on Christmas morning.

"He loves to play on his tractors and in his trucks. Even though he's working, he calls it playing, because he has so much fun with it," Mary said. "Doug is working his dream job. He's doing what he was meant to do."

Happy fathers day
Pa Pa Youve ben good to
me these years.
Remember I hope you
don't die. I love you.
love Brent

6-19-2005

Above: Doug poses with his sister, Doris Stamey. He has two other sisters not pictured here, Dorothy, who is now deceased, and Helen.

Below: Grandson Brent Chandler, 10, loves his "Papa" and wants to one day have his own grading and hauling business. This is a letter he wrote Doug in 2005.

Mary, who says "it was love at first sight" when she first met Doug on a blind date over forty-three years ago, is not the only family member working in the business. The still-growing company also employs son Lamar Tench, son-in-law Donald Anderson and grandson Ronnie Anderson. Another son, Marty, worked with his father for years before going out on his own, and one of their grandsons, Brent Chandler, ten, can hardly wait to grow up and help his "papa".

"When Brent comes to visit from Alabama and gets near a tractor, his eyes glaze over just like Doug's always have," Mary said with a laugh.

All told, Mary and Doug have 7 children, 17 grandchildren, and 8 great grandchildren. When they do find a little spare time, they enjoy spending time with family and traveling.

As for the future, it looks like the Tenchs are right where they want to be. In fact, when asked if he has ever considered retiring, Tench had this to say: "Nope, I don't plan on retiring anytime soon, not as long as I can go. Even if I won the lottery tomorrow, I don't think I'd stop working. I might take a little time off, do a little more traveling with Mary, but then I'd come home and buy some more tractors," he laughed.

"He tries to sound like he's joking, but that's exactly what he'd do," Mary said with a smile. "That's exactly what he'd do."

For more information about D.W. Tench Hauling and Grading, you can reach Doug or Mary at the same number they have had for the past forty-seven-years—770-457-5306—or email them at M.tench@attglobal.net.

Handy & General Hardware

✧

Above: Harold D. Smith and son, Joseph.

Below: Joe, Harold, Jr., and Matthew Smith, current owners of Handy & General Store.

The Smith family history runs deep in DeKalb, and for over seventy years the name has been best known for being behind county hardware stores where you find not only quality service and merchandise, but more importantly, items you will not find any place else.

"The philosophy of our operations always has been to serve the needs of the customer no matter how small or large the need may be," said Joe Smith, present owner and operator along with two of his sons, of the family's two stores—Handy Ace Hardware and General Hardware. Smith is the son of the late Harold D. Smith, who founded the first Smith Hardware store in 1935 in Depression-era DeKalb after he had gained fifteen years of experience working for Atlanta's nationally known Beck and Gregg Wholesale Hardware Supply Company.

The Smith family legacy goes back to the 1800s in DeKalb. Harold's father, Robert Franklin Smith, who died in 1940, was a prominent farmer, school teacher, and state legislator.

The first Smith Hardware, which opened on East College Avenue in Decatur, quickly gained a reputation where you could find that hard-to-get item. "His motto was, 'If we don't have it, we'll get it' no matter how large or small it may be," son Joe said of his father's philosophy. After nearly eight decades it remains the Smith Hardware motto.

Realizing there would be some demand for items from a quickly passing era and in keeping with his tradition of always having hard-to-find items, in the early 1950s Smith purchased all of Sears-Roebuck distribution center's remaining inventory of mule plows, harnesses, and leather goods, which was sold over a twenty-year period. These were mostly leather goods made locally at the Bona Allen Company in Buford, Georgia.

When the East College store opened, an array of the not-so-hard-to-find items on display were horse collars, cotton scales, pitch forks, and iron skillets. It was around 1955 when Smith Hardware sold the last new horse-drawn carriage in the county.

Over the years the store, which eventually expanded from its original 2.000-square-foot space to more than 25,000 square feet, became both a DeKalb landmark and institution where shoppers from all over the county and the surrounding area came to get their hardware items.

When founder Harold died in 1957, his son, Joe, was a junior at the University of Georgia. Joe came home to help run the business and finished his education at Atlanta's Georgia State University. He remembers many loyal employees who worked with his father and who helped him make the transition from student to store owner. They included James Bailey, Charlie Rohrer, Duke Glass, and Freddie Freeman. Freeman was store manager and eventually opened his own store, Freeman's Hardware on Memorial Drive in DeKalb, which became a mini-version of Smith's "hard-to-find items" type store.

"There were many loyal co-workers who helped make the College Avenue store a success," Joe pointed out. They included longtime manager Ottis Phillips, Logan Thomas, T. W. Robinson, Tom Sullivan, Jeanette Thompson, Bill Davis, Kenneth Elam, Ronnie Smith, and founder Harold Smith's brother, Temple.

Another Smith Hardware motto is "always be prepared", which means stocking items in the event of unlikely emergencies, such as local, infrequent ice storms. That philosophy was tested to the limit in the early 1970s when two ice storms hit DeKalb and metro

Atlanta hard, only a year apart. "We always try to be prepared for weather related emergencies," Joe said. "But ice storms in '71 and '73 sent us scrambling to find anything that would provide heat and light because the power was out for days in both storms." Stoves, gas and oil heaters, and lanterns were in great demand and both Smith Hardware stores searched all over the state in an effort to find these much needed items for their customers. "We sent trucks as far away as Augusta with orders to fill them up," he said. Both employees and customers were bundled up because there was no heat. "We served our customers from dawn to dark when the only light we had was from skylights and lanterns", Joe proudly remembers.

After eighteen years of operating the College Avenue store, due to health problems Joe decided it was time to take a break from the hardware store business. But the hardware business was in his blood, and he spent the next three years traveling the state selling specialty hardware items to local hardware dealers. "It kept me up-to-date," Joe said, "and gave me some new ideas about the business."

In the late 1970s his brother-in-law, longtime and well-known DeKalb businessman Walter Austin convinced Joe that the Brookhaven area of DeKalb needed a good hardware store. So, in 1977 he bought a former "Austin Washmobile" on Peachtree Road in Brookhaven from Austin and opened General Hardware.

General Hardware's first store manager, Tom Hutton, had worked for Joe at the Decatur Smith Hardware when he was a teenager.

Two years after the store opened the Austins, Walter and Joe's sister, Sarah, purchased an interest in the business. Later on Eddie Huff, a former manager at Austin Washmobile, became store manager. The current manager is Ben Fortenberry.

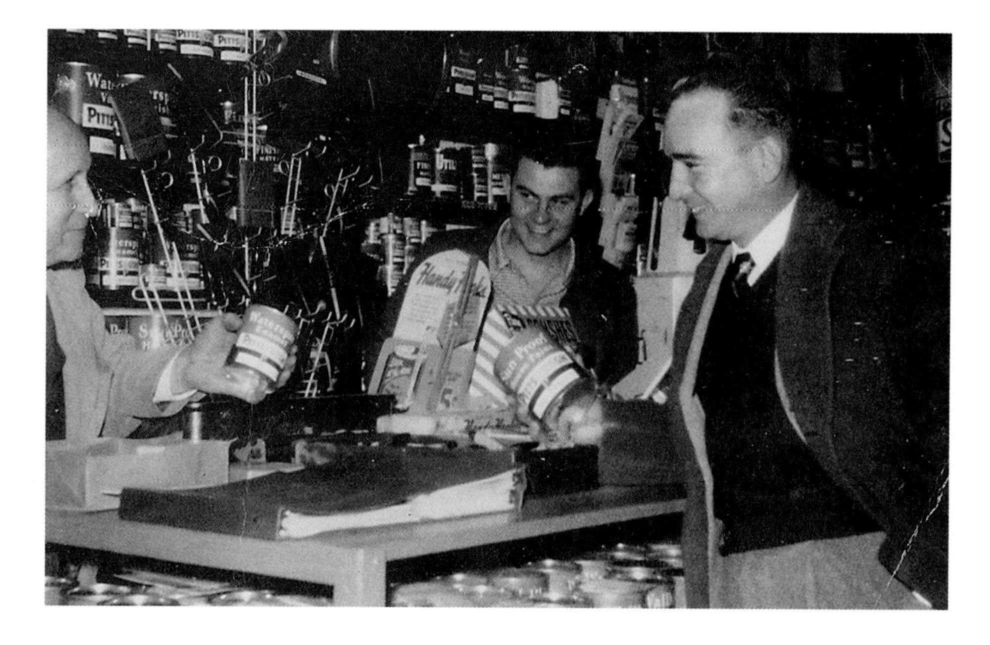

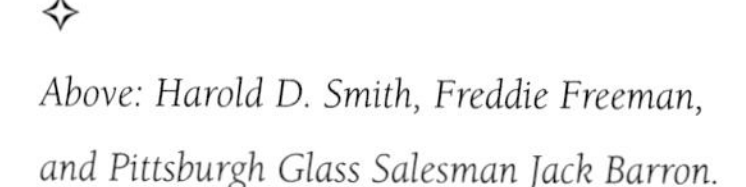

Above: Harold D. Smith, Freddie Freeman, and Pittsburgh Glass Salesman Jack Barron.

✧

Above: Joseph Smith, son of Harold D. Smith.

Below: Harold D. Smith, owner of Smith Hardware.

In 1983, Ottis Phillips, the former manager of the Decatur Smith Hardware, contacted Joe about the possibility of finding another hardware business to buy. The result was the purchase of a former King Hardware store in Tucker, which at the time was owned by longtime DeKalb Hardware store operator George Warren who had renamed it Handy Ace Hardware. The store quickly outgrew its location on Lawrenceville Highway and was moved to its present location on Hugh Howell Road in Tucker, which was a former Big Apple grocery store. In the past two decades the store has shown strong, steady growth, becoming a must stop for those shopping for a wide variety of hardware items. You often hear the expression, "If you can't find it anywhere else, you can find it at Handy." It has grown from 8,500 square feet to more than 36,000 square feet and plans for further expansion to meet growing demand are being studied. Gary Watson, a long-time Handy Hardware staff member, is current store manager.

In 1988, J. Harold Smith, Jr., Joe's oldest son, became the third generation of Smiths to become part of store management after he graduated from Georgia Southern University. "The one common denominator of all the stories I've heard about my grandfather was his devotion to providing service second to none with a desire for complete customer satisfaction. That's what we are still doing today," he commented. "Although today's hardware business environment has changed drastically with the addition of the big boxes, (Home Depot and Lowes) there still seems to be great demand for a business that

has the philosophy which was instilled in the family by my grandfather and father."

In an unusual venture for a hardware store, Joe recalls the time when Smith Hardware was awarded the contract to provide the dynamite and blasting caps to assist in the construction of the mammoth Buford Dam on Lake Lanier. The original Smith Hardware also stocked dynamite and blasting caps for retail sale.

Up until the 1960s the hardware distribution process was maintained through wholesale distributors. In Atlanta the wholesale distributors were Beck & Gregg Hardware, Sharp Horsey Hardware, Dinkins Davidson Hardware, Pittsburg Plate Glass, and Peaslee Gaulbert Hardware. Other wholesalers not in the Atlanta area included Lovett & Thorpe, Belknap Hardware, and Shopleigh Hardware. All of these wholesale distributors have since closed their doors.

In these days, before the advent of computers, a salesman usually dressed eloquently, would have a specific territory and specific day of the week he would come by to see if the retailer had any needs in the way of product or information pertaining to the goods he represented. For the most part these 'outside sales reps' have vanished. Computers now make it easier to track down new products and catalogs are either on a CD/DVD or on-line in a PDF file.

Today, retailers are responsible for the merchandise mix in their stores based upon the needs of his particular market or customer. The void of the wholesalers and the sales reps has been filled by hardware co-ops such as Ace Hardware and Tru-Serv. These hardware co-ops are merely a way for a group of retailers to pool their resources together for the sole purpose of achieving better pricing and a better product mix than could be achieved independently. Product offering is strictly based on the demand of the customer, whatever the product may be.

Matthew Smith, Harold's youngest brother who also is imbued with a deep knowledge of the business, is also active in the company stores. When they were growing up, Smith's other children, Laurie, Sundi, and Eric worked in the business becoming imbued with the Smith Hardware legacy, memories which they cherish today.

Now, a fourth generation of Smiths works part-time summer jobs at the business and are poised to take their places to carry on the Smith tradition and legacy when the time comes.

✧

Above: Duke Glass, an employee proud to always wear his apron.

Below: A buggy ordered for a customer.

Wesley Woods

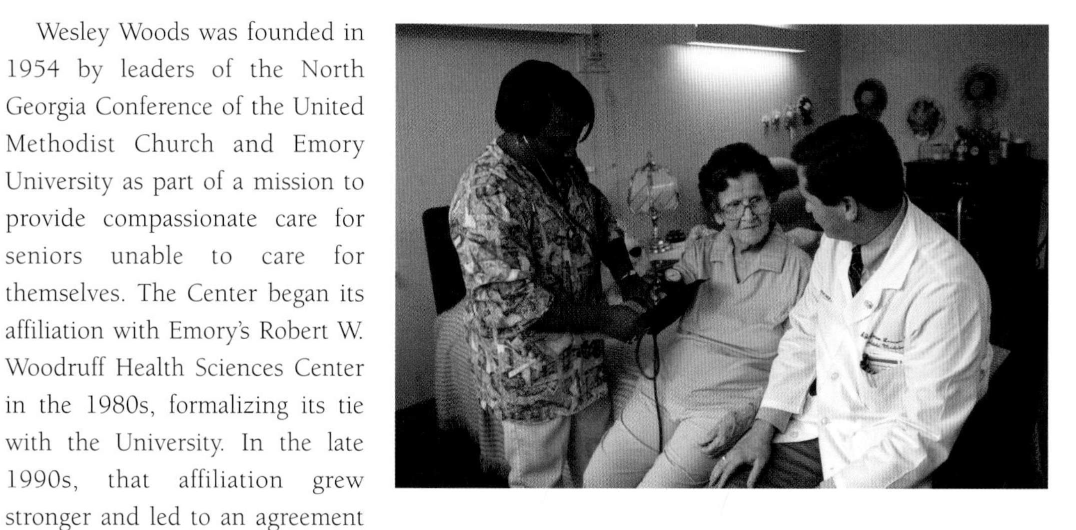

Wesley Woods was founded in 1954 by leaders of the North Georgia Conference of the United Methodist Church and Emory University as part of a mission to provide compassionate care for seniors unable to care for themselves. The Center began its affiliation with Emory's Robert W. Woodruff Health Sciences Center in the 1980s, formalizing its tie with the University. In the late 1990s, that affiliation grew stronger and led to an agreement under which nearby Wesley Woods Center came under Emory's umbrella. Out of this grew the Wesley Woods Center of Emory University, where interdisciplinary training, research and treatment programs comprise one of the most comprehensive approaches to issues of geriatrics in the United States today.

Located a mile and a half from Emory University Hospital on a sixty-four acre wooded campus in Atlanta's Druid Hills neighborhood, Wesley Woods Center is nationally recognized for its comprehensive care for individuals and families who face age-related healthcare issues. The Center is comprised of Wesley Woods Geriatric Hospital, Wesley Woods Long Term Hospital, Wesley Woods Outpatient Clinic, Budd Terrace nursing care facility, Wesley Woods Towers and the Wesley Woods Health Center. One of only a handful of geriatric centers in the United States, Wesley Woods Center and the dedicated staff provide hope, help and care to older adults throughout Georgia and the Southeast.

Wesley Woods Center is not just a campus of buildings, but also a campus of people who are dedicated to compassionate care of senior adults. The facility provides cutting edge care and research and has a hand in developing how senior care will be provided in the future not just in Georgia but throughout the country. The Center was founded on a belief that we can provide better care for seniors in our area—a belief that has continued to develop and mature over the years.

The first building to open was Wesley Woods Towers in 1965. One of only a few retirement living options in the area at the time, the Towers were the first round buildings constructed in Atlanta. This offered the campus a trademark look but also demonstrated the forward thinking and vision Wesley Woods had for retirement living. The circular design provides residents with an optimal living experience. The round shape of each building also allows the 201 apartments to be organized into "neighborhoods," providing the residents a sense of community essential to good health at any age. In 2005, Wesley Woods Towers celebrated its fortieth anniversary. Today, the staff continues to encourage the residents to experience the many riches later life has to offer.

Above: Located a mile and a half from Emory University Hospital, Wesley Woods Center is nationally recognized for its comprehensive care for individuals and families who face age-related healthcare issues.

PHOTOGRAPH COURTESY OF BILLY HOWARD.

Below: Dr. W. Candler Budd, the driving force behind the Wesley Woods movement and board member, Mrs. J.C. Malone, break ground on May 22, 1963, for the first home, Wesley Woods Towers.

As the retirement housing division of Wesley Woods, Wesley Woods Senior Living, Inc., and affiliates owns and manages the sister communities of Wesley Woods providing independent apartment and cottage living, assisted living, nursing care and Alzheimer's care at eight locations throughout North Georgia. It is affiliated with both the North Georgia Conference of the United Methodist Church and Wesley Woods Center. A nonprofit organization, Wesley Woods Senior Living communities provide comprehensive, regionally oriented programs and serve as training and research facilities to address important health issues associated with aging.

As time passed, Wesley Woods' leadership recognized that skilled nursing care would be a pressing need for its residents living in the Towers as well as in the surrounding community. Out of that need grew the Wesley Woods Health Center, which was completed in 1967. The Health Center provided skilled nursing care and treatment to restore patients to their former living arrangements, as well as long-term care for patients unable to return home. The Health Center was home to a number of prominent Atlantans, including Lena Fox whose life served as a basis for a play and subsequently, the Academy Award-winning movie "Driving Miss Daisy."

The building is now home to the Emory Center for Health in Aging, an interdisciplinary training and research center used by the Emory Schools of Medicine, Nursing and Public Health. Through the Emory Center for Health in Aging, Wesley Woods Center and Emory University are working together along with nineteen other academic medical facilities throughout the United States to develop better teaching methods for future geriatricians.

The Health Center is also home to Emory researchers focusing on movement disorders,

✧

Above: Wesley Woods utilizes horticultural therapy as part of our rehabilitation program.

PHOTOGRAPH COURTESY OF BILLY HOWARD.

Below: Emory researchers in the Wesley Woods Health Center are working diligently in the areas of movement disorders, Alzheimer's disease and neurology to provide better care to today's seniors as well as future seniors.

PHOTOGRAPH COURTESY OF BILLY HOWARD.

Alzheimer's disease and neurology. In 2007 a research neuro-imaging center was constructed on the second floor of the building to assist Emory scientists in these areas of research. Other clinics in the building include the Fuqua Center for Late-Life Depression, the Emory Sleep Center, an outpatient geriatric psychiatry practice and a geriatric dentist. At any one time, there are more than 150 physicians, researchers and/or nurses working together to discover new treatments, provide top-quality care and develop new medical techniques for seniors.

As the campus continued to develop, leadership decided an intermediate-care facility was needed. Budd Terrace, named in honor of Dr. Candler Budd, one of those responsible for bringing to fruition a ministry to older adults in the North Georgia Conference, was opened as an assisted living facility in 1972. Built to accommodate 200 people, it became one of the first free standing, intermediate-care units in the Southeast.

Budd Terrace provides long-term care and sub-acute care to Atlanta seniors. As this population has grown, Budd Terrace has evolved to meet the new demands of this older and frailer population. Residents and visitors notice a difference when they enter the building. Friendly greetings, warm smiles, a cheerful staff and genuine, caring attitudes are a vital aspect of the care provided at Budd Terrace. The facility has been undergoing renovations over the past few years in an effort to continue delivering quality care to Atlanta seniors. In 2006 inpatient hospice services were added to the list of services offered at Budd Terrace.

Above: Wesley Woods Center residents and patients enjoy the wooded scenery of the sixty-four acre campus.

Below: Budd Terrace provides long-term care and sub-acute care to Atlanta seniors.

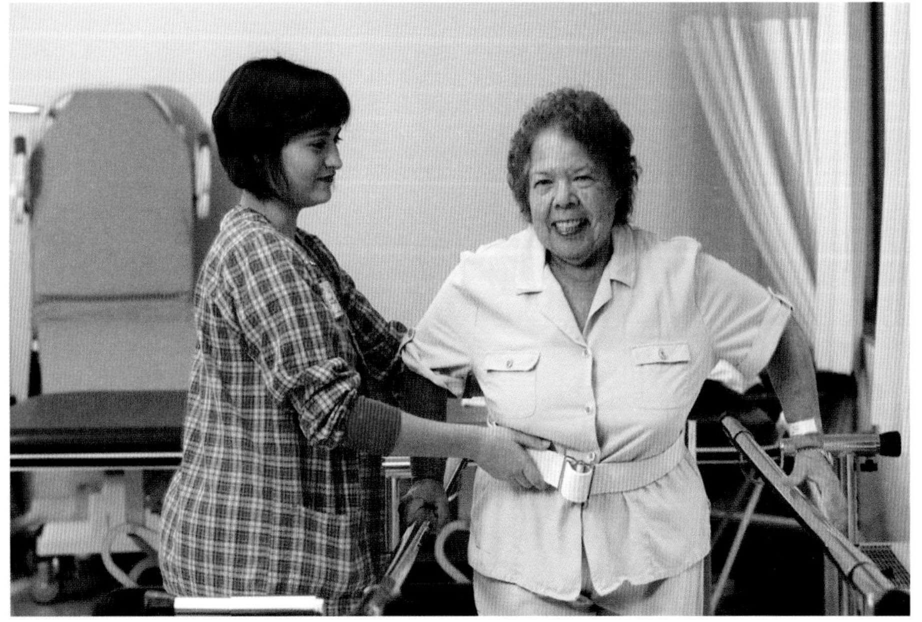

In order for the campus to provide care for every aspect of elder adults' needs, one piece of the healthcare puzzle was missing. In September 1985, ground was broken for the $20 million, 100-bed Wesley Woods Geriatric Teaching and Research Hospital. This was the first free-standing geriatric hospital in the nation. The stated goals of the hospital are to diagnose and treat medical and psychiatric disorders affecting older adults, to develop models for geriatric services and educational resources and to broaden Wesley Woods' commitment to charitable care.

The prize-winning architectural design for the geriatric hospital creates a non-institutional feel, with low exterior lines topped with gabled roofs and each patient room opening onto a living-room-like space. The two-story hospital features an outpatient clinic, inpatient and outpatient rehabilitation services, long term acute care, a medical unit and two secure inpatient psychiatric units. This hospital, like all other facilities on the Wesley Woods Center campus, specializes in serving the fastest

growing segment of the population in the United States—aging adults.

Each year, the Foundation of Wesley Woods provides millions of dollars worth of unreimbursed care with support from generous donors and foundations. As a not-for-profit geriatric hospital and primary care clinic, your contributions are critical to keeping our doors open. The Foundation of Wesley Woods was created to ensure that healthcare services remain available to seniors in Georgia. Every day, the Foundation of Wesley Woods works to make possible health, comfort and dignity in the lives of older adults, especially for those whose lifetime savings does not stretch far enough, for those whose health problems have left them physically and financially depleted, and for those who are alone.

The funds raised for charitable care replace reimbursement shortfalls and allow older adults who are unable to pay for treatment to continue to receive the care that they need. Additionally, the Foundation's donors provide funds for the upkeep and renovation of our retirement communities, helping to ensure that Wesley Woods continues to provide the high quality residential services that our residents deserve. They also enable us to provide special care for patients suffering from Alzheimer's disease, Parkinson's disease and age-related depression. To make a donation, please contact the Foundation of Wesley Woods at 404-728-6381.

Wesley Woods Center's commitment to leadership in the treatment and research of age-related healthcare issues continues today. With the looming baby boomer bubble about to burst, elder care will become a priority for more people than ever before. Wesley Woods Geriatric Hospital and Primary Care Clinics are unique in their sole treatment of diseases affecting older adults. In the past five years, the dedicated staff has provided care to more than 145,000 older adults. Almost two-thirds of our patients travel here from outside of Atlanta. In 2005, forty-six percent of all Georgia Medicare patients diagnosed with degenerative nervous system disorders—primarily Alzheimer and Parkinson's diseases—were treated at the Wesley Woods Geriatric Hospital.

Above: In September 1985, ground was broken for the $20-million Wesley Woods Geriatric Hospital. This was the first freestanding geriatric hospital in the nation.

Below: The Foundation of Wesley Woods was created to ensure that healthcare services remain available to seniors in Georgia.

DeKalb County Public Library

The rich history of libraries in DeKalb County had its genesis in Lithonia in 1907 when Miss Lula Almand gathered books in her home and invited local citizens to freely read and borrow. Later the local Woman's Club, where Miss Lula was a charter member, founded the Lithonia Public Library, which today serves as a branch of the DeKalb County Public Library (DCPL).

In 1925 the Decatur Library, which was the forerunner of the DeKalb County Public Library, was founded when a group of citizens led by Mrs. William Saywood and Mrs. William Alden met to form a Public Library Association. The first board of directors was, besides Mrs. Saywood and Mrs. Alden, Charles D. McKinney, Mrs. John DeSaussure, William Jones, G. W. Glausier, and J. A. Hall. Part-time Decatur librarians, who served until 1930 when Mrs. A. B. "Maud" Burrus was named the first full-time librarian, were Mrs. W. Z. Paulie, Miss Anna Harwell, and Miss Grace Kehrer.

Commenting on the work of Burrus and early library leaders, Murphey Candler, prominent local lawyer and editor of the *DeKalb New Era*, wrote, ..."Besides the work of Mrs. Burrus who is literally devoting her life to the cultural advancement of our county, and who through her efforts has placed the Decatur Library Association high in the ranks of libraries throughout the state, the work of Mrs. Alden, Mrs. Sayward, and Dr. D. P. McGeachy has been outstanding."

The DeKalb County Public Library has a history of strong, capable directors, beginning with its first bona fide librarian in 1930, Burrus, who served for thirty-one years. She was succeeded by her assistant director Louise Trotti in 1961, and in 1982 Barbara Loar, who had served as assistant to Trotti, was named to succeed her. When Loar retired in 1991, assistant director Donna Mancini was appointed to succeed her. She resigned in 1995 to accept another position, and Darro Willey was named as library director.

The Decatur Library began operating a "county wide division" in the 1930s, and supported twenty-five book depositories in private homes around DeKalb County. In 1938 the Lithonia Public Library was added as a branch and a major milestone in 1940 was the operation of DCPL's first bookmobile, funded by the Roosevelt administration's Work Progress Administration (WPA). The idea for a bookmobile was born when Burrus began taking books in the back of her car to readers in the small towns and farms throughout the county. The first supervisor of bookmobile services was Burrus' later successor, Trotti. In 1952 a new "Library on Wheels" was purchased, and the older 1940 vintage vehicle was reconditioned to serve African Americans in rural DeKalb County.

The Library's original home was in the Decatur Bank & Trust Company building, and it was later moved to City Hall where it remained until a new library building,

Above: Director Maud Burrus with the Decatur Library's first bookmobile, 1948.

Below: Director Maud Burrus (1930-1961) at the dedication of the Decatur Public Library (1950). County Commissioner Scott Candler is the third person from the right.

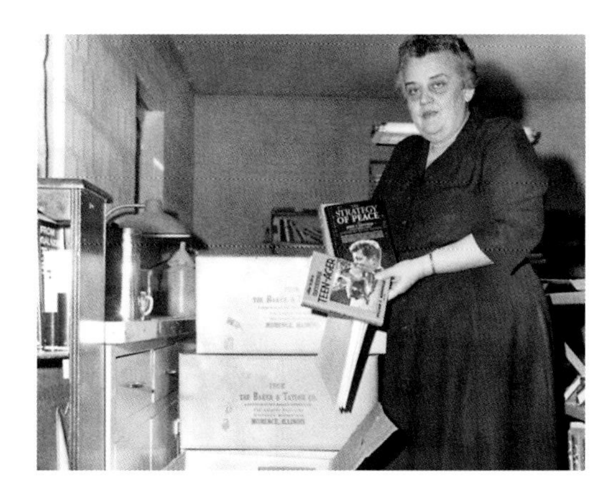

following separate Decatur and DeKalb bond issues, was built at a cost of $180,000 on Sycamore Street in 1950. The site of the new library was bequeathed to the city by Annie Scott Cooper as a memorial to her father, George Washington Scott, founder of Agnes Scott College and to her husband, Thomas L. Cooper, who had served on the Library's Board of Directors. The Library was renamed the Decatur-DeKalb Library. The building quickly became too small and an addition was built in 1954 to house an auditorium and the Fine Arts and Cataloging Departments. In 1962 the building was renamed the Maud M. Burrus Library following Burrus' retirement.

From 1938 to 1962 in then segregated DeKalb County, library service to African Americans was provided through the Carver Branch Library operated in the Herring Street School as a cooperative effort with the Decatur Board of Education. This segregated library service quietly came to an end in DeKalb County in 1962, when Elizabeth Wilson and her daughter registered for and received library cards at the Decatur Library. Wilson later became the first woman and African American to be elected mayor of Decatur.

The Decatur-DeKalb Library became a regional library with the affiliation of Rockdale County in 1951 and Newton County in 1953. In 1962 the library was renamed the DeKalb Library System. In 1989, DeKalb County withdrew from the regional library effectively dissolving it. By this time the populations of both Rockdale and Newton Counties had grown to the point where they could operate as separate county libraries. The DeKalb Library System then became the DeKalb County Public Library, as it is known today.

The library system received considerable notoriety in 1983, when it became the first library in Georgia, and possibly the nation, to adopt the national blue-and-white library symbol into a series of directional signs on state and national roadways in DeKalb County directing drivers to nearby library branches.

From its first city and county bond issues in the late forties, which built the original 1950 building, funds from bond elections have been vital to the Library's growth. None was more important than the 1986 bond issue, which funded expansions or replacements of four existing county library facilities, including the Decatur Library, as well as eleven new library branches. Commenting on its importance, Barbara Loar, Library Director at the time, said, "We were almost overwhelmed by the thought of an expansion that would nearly double the size of the library system and more than double the number of books we had."

When the Library was reopened in 1992 after being in temporary quarters on the Decatur Square, it was renamed the Decatur Library as a City of Decatur requirement for its site donation, and the fourth floor of the addition was named the Maud M. Burrus Administrative office; however, many long time residents still affectionately refer to the building as the Maud Burrus Library The original 1950 building remains incorporated in the present Decatur Library.

Among those instrumental in passing this watershed bond issue were DCPL Library

✧

Above: Director (1961-1981) and Assistant Director (1952-1961) Louise Trotti.

Below: Book Week Program at Carver Branch Library, 1953.

✧

Above: The Decatur Library serves as the headquarters for the DeKalb County Public Library.

Below: Director (1982-1991) and Assistant Director (1971-1982) Barbara Loar.

Trustee Thurbert Baker, now Georgia's Attorney General, and Library Trustee Jenny McCurdy, who were co-chairs of the effort. Library Trustees Jane Norcross and William C. Brown also played vital roles in the bond issue. Worthy of special note, both McCurdy and Norcross were awarded the American Library Association's highest citation for library trustees for their work both in DeKalb County and nationally.

The library system is now undergoing a similar expansion in the wake of a 2005 County Bond Election, which authorized $54,540,000 for the construction of five replacement library facilities, four expanded and renovated libraries, and three new libraries, bringing the number of DCPL facilities to twenty-six. Library Board Chair Herb Sprague led the 2005 campaign for the library system, which resulted in the library bond proposal receiving the highest vote count of three bond proposals on the ballot, the others being Parks and Transportation.

The DeKalb County Public Library has long been a state and national leader in the development of innovative programs, and that tradition continues today. One of the Library's most visible and popular programs is its Georgia Center for the Book (GCB), which supports Georgia's rich literary heritage. The Center, as the state affiliate of the Library of Congress, has been hosted and funded by DCPL since late 1997. Under this banner the library system has supported a number of statewide literary programs, including the Georgia Literary Festival (held in a different Georgia community each year), the All Georgia Reads program (which selects one book every two years for all Georgians to read), and the sponsorship of every major literary award given in Georgia. The Center for the Book program has made DCPL the largest literary program presenter in the Southeast United States, with over 100 author programs currently being presented annually. Through its GCB operation, the library system was also a co-founder of the *Atlanta Journal Constitution*/Decatur Book Festival, which has recorded annual attendance of over 50,000 persons.

For those residents who have a need for literacy skills, DCPL's unique Project REAP (Reading Empowers All People) has been invaluable. This innovative program, utilizing Library resources and personnel, has taught hundreds of immigrant families, adults, and children Basic English skills since 1999. Its impact has affected the lives of thousands, sometimes in unexpected ways. It started with a private donation to the DeKalb Library Foundation to help promote immigrant and refugee family literacy. Since its inception, it has grown, expanded, and changed, yet never lost its focus on helping people develop skills to improve their lives. DCPL offers classes outside the Library and hosts visits at local libraries where parents and their children can obtain library cards, browse collections, including materials in their first language, and attend special programs.

In addition to Project REAP, the Library has partnered with literacy providers for English as a Second Language (ESOL) classes in county libraries, and has developed special literacy collections in sixteen branches to support other literacy provider programs. DCPL currently partners with Literacy Volunteers of America, Literacy Action, the Latin American Association, and DeKalb Technical College in on-going literacy efforts.

DeKalb's diversity, stemming from the second largest increase of immigrant population of any metropolitan area in the nation over a ten year period (according to the Center for Immigrant Studies), has added to the richness of the county's culture. Providing library services for that kind of diversity has proved a formidable, continuing challenge.

Because DCPL's multicultural population also includes a majority of African-American residents, the library system features many programs directed toward this clientele. Among the Library's most widely praised and anticipated programs is its annual Kwanzaa Awareness Festival. Such programs were relatively rare in the 1980s, when longtime library manager Doris Wells introduced them at DCPL. Today, this ever-growing series of programs, author visits, and activities commemorates a holiday central to the lives and culture of many Library patrons.

Of special note is DCPL's groundbreaking "Building Blocks" program, an informal recreational and educational project that began in 1992 at the Redan-Trotti Library. Initially this interactive program focused on low-literate teen parents fifteen through eighteen years old and their children from birth through thirty-six months. In 1994, "Building Blocks" was recognized by the American Library Association in its listing of "Excellence in Library Services to Young Adults." This popular program continues today, introducing all parents and their children to activities and materials which enhance the development of infant language and motor skills.

DCPL currently operates twenty-two library branches spread over the county's 268 square miles and a Library Processing Center. As a result of a 2005 Bond Issue, this will increase to twenty-six facilities by 2010. The library collection is approaching 1,000,000 items, and over 200,000 county residents have active library cards. Annual circulation in 2007 was 3.5 million with library visits reaching a record 3.3 million people. Nearly twice as many people used DPCL facilities in 2007 as attended Atlanta Falcons, Thrashers, and Hawks home games combined in the same year. Since 2000 the circulation of library materials has risen forty-eight percent, belying predictions that public libraries are an endangered species.

A random public telephone survey conducted by outside consultants in 2000 revealed that DeKalb County citizens believed that among county agencies, the library provided the best value. Quarterly surveys since then repeatedly show ninety-eight percent satisfaction levels among regular library users. Accompanying DCPL's spring 2005 nomination for the Georgia Governor's Award in the Humanities (which it subsequently received), many library patrons eagerly took up pen to proclaim their feelings about the organization: "The DeKalb County Public Library has demonstrated vision and commitment," wrote State Representative Stephanie S. Benfield, Democrat-Decatur.

Above: Left to Right: Library Trustee Curtis Branscome (1997-2008); Library Trustee Eleanor Duke (2008); Library Trustee Mary Lee Davis (1998-2008) and Library Director Darro Willey (1995-2008) at the groundbreaking ceremony for the construction of a new Toco Hill-Avis G. Williams Library Branch, 2008.

Bottom, left: Director (1991-1995) and Assistant Director (1982-1991) Donna Mancini and Library Trustee William C. Brown (1976-1990).

Bottom, right: DeKalb County Public Library staff at Staff Development Day 2005.

H&A International Jewelry, Ltd.

H&A International Jewelry, Ltd. began in DeKalb twenty-five years ago as a small diamond importer and wholesaler and today is a full service jeweler serving an international clientele.

The company has a complete manufacturing and fabrication facility capable of custom making virtually any piece of jewelry and also maintains a large variety of inventory.

Over the past two and one-half decades the business has been built on a combination of exceptional customer service and comparatively small mark-ups on the highest quality merchandise. "Small mark ups," owner and founder Haim Haviv says, "along with rapport, responsibility, and honesty with our clients, are the keys to our success."

Longtime client Randy Galanti says, "H&A is open to the public by referral, and in the last decade I've purchased watches, earrings, pearls and diamonds, not only because of the dollar value Haviv offers, but because I feel like family whenever I walk through the door."

A jeweler of the highest repute, Haviv continues to widen his circle of friends and customers. "I've run into only one problem in my dealings with H&A," client Nan White says. "I don't have enough fingers, toes, wrists or ears." Haviv's success speaks for itself—once a customer, always a customer at H&A International Jewelry.

Above: Haim Haviv inspects polished diamonds at Dunwoody office.

Below: Diamonds in the rough—overseas stones on display for purchase.

When he came to the U.S. from his native Israel in 1978 to attend business school in Los Angeles, Haviv became fascinated with the diamond industry and its place in the U.S. market. The next year he visited Atlanta and immediately decided it was the place to be. "I loved it," Haviv enthused, "It's a wonderful location with a great quality of life, and for a businessman the airport is a great asset."

Haviv found a job with one of Atlanta's leading jewelers at the time, Ellmans, and worked there for two years. "I realized while working at Ellmans that I could make a real contribution to the community by bringing a true diamond wholesaler to Atlanta," he said. "Israel has one of the largest diamond exchanges in the world. Being born there and speaking the language, I realized I could communicate better than anyone else here at the time." Thus, H&A International was born. The company opened its doors in 1982 and was officially incorporated the next year.

H&A quickly gained the reputation as the place to go for quality merchandise for the best price. Through word of mouth and personal referrals the company experienced steady growth. "We began to build a large client base and have made sure to maintain it by dealing honestly and responsibly," Haviv emphasized.

Haviv makes frequent trips to Israel, Belgium and other parts of the world, maintaining contacts that provide his company with some of the top quality gems available on the market. Through ventures with major diamond cutters in Israel and Belgium, H&A can obtain any size and quality diamond at the best possible price and is an authorized dealer for international designers and notable name brands, such as A. Jaffe, Alex Primak, Diana, Verragio, Fusaro, Doris Panos, Hidalgo, Raymond Weil, Concord, and Movado.

Since 1986, H&A has been located in its two story headquarters in Independence Square in DeKalb's upscale Dunwoody community. It is an international destination with merchants flying in from all over the world to buy a variety of gems.

In his native Israel, Haviv served as a Navy officer, and now he serves his adopted country as a captain in Georgia's State Army Guard.

Both H&A and the Haviv family are actively involved in local civic and charitable events and causes. The Havivs host an annual champagne-and-diamonds fundraiser to benefit Hospice, and are actively involved with supporting many of Atlanta's private Jewish schools and local sporting events at the Jewish Community Center. The company supports many charitable causes, such as the American Cancer Society.

Through his business Haviv has become close friends with many of his celebrity clients who enthusiastically give testimonials on behalf of him and the company. As an example, Hall of Fame quarterback Fran Tarkenton spotlighted Haviv as one of his "favorite" small business entrepreneurs in his best selling book on small businesses. Another example of close knit friendships with a friend and client is when Haviv was best man at the wedding of Oakland Raiders' football great, Lincoln Kennedy. Nationally syndicated radio economic guru Clark Howard extols the virtues of H&A and its owner. Former Atlanta Falcons' coach Dan Reeves is both a close friend and client. Atlanta Braves pitching ace John Smoltz is the official company spokesman.

✧

Above: Haviv has five children (four of whom are pictured here with their father) Eric, Kevin, Max, Amalia, and the newest addition to the family, Gabriella, whom he would like see become involved with the business.

Below: Owner and Founder Haim Haviv.

EPPS AVIATION

The history of Epps Aviation is a family affair, which epitomizes the history of aviation in DeKalb. Pat Epps, whose father Ben was a pioneering pilot credited with being Georgia's first aviator, founded the company forty-two years ago at DeKalb Peachtree Airport (PDK). Today, with his three children, Elaine, Marian, and Patrick, Jr., he runs the largest fixed-base operation (FBO) in Georgia at PDK.

From a small company selling fuel and providing aircraft maintenance, Epps has grown into a twenty-one acre complex with six corporate hangars and forty T-hangars providing a vast array of services including charter, aircraft sales and management, avionics, maintenance and tie-down space for local and visiting aircraft.

Among services Epps has provided to a nationwide clientele for the past four decades is a fleet of Jet and Turbo-Prop aircraft available twenty-four hours a day. Company pilots are qualified to land at virtually any airport, domestically or internationally. Known for its "red carpet" treatment, Epps offers round the clock fuel service, hotel reservations and catering.

Epps maintains an extensive parts and equipment inventory and, something unusual for an air service of its kind, a vast research library. With more than $1 million of test equipment and spares, the company is an authorized service center for Cessna, Mitsubishi and Pilatus and for all major avionics manufacturers.

As a mark of its esteem in the industry, Epps is one of the few independent FBOs routinely named to *Professional Pilot Magazine*'s list of best FBOs in the nation. It also has been named the South's premier corporate and general aviation facility.

Above: Pat Epps.

Below: Buried beneath the ice cap for fifty years, this vintage P-38 fighter plane was retrieved on Epps' Greenland Expedition.

PHOTO 1992 © LOU SAPIENZA/GES.

Today, the company, stronger than ever, is an industry leader. "In recent times the air transportation industry has seen the introduction of aircraft management companies and the invention of fractional ownership companies," says Epps.

Following in the footsteps of his famous father who began barnstorming over the state in aircraft of his own design in the early 1900's, Pat is an accomplished pilot who still flies his signature red, white and blue Aerobatic Beechcraft Bonanza in local air shows.

One of his oldest customers and friends, Charles Loudermilk, Atlanta civic and business leader and founder of Aaron Rents, calls Pat "the king of all pilots." Loudermilk has had planes at Epps Aviation for the past forty years. "DeKalb Peachtree would not be the airport it is without Pat," he says. "He has been the driving force behind growth and progress at PDK."

"Pat is one of the most personable people you will ever meet and he really takes care of his customers," Loudermilk adds.

The two old friends are longtime members of the Rotary club and are very much involved in state and local politics. "Pat is not only one of Georgia's aviation pioneers, he is one of our most civic minded citizens," Loudermilk concluded.

The passion for flight Pat inherited from Ben has been passed on to his three children

who are all pilots. Carrying on the family tradition after the tragic death of her husband Ben in a takeoff crash in 1937 in Athens, the matriarch of the family, Omie Williams Epps supported the efforts of her nine children to fly. Eight became pilots.

After graduating from Georgia Tech in 1956, Pat married his high school sweetheart, Ann Hailey, and took a job with Boeing Airplane Company in Seattle as a flight test engineer on the prototype 707. In 1958 he completed Air Force pilot training, serving until 1963 as a transport pilot on several different multi-engine models. Starting part-time in 1964 selling Mooney Aircraft, he opened Epps Aviation in 1965.

Epps inherited his father's pioneering spirit, resourcefulness and perseverance—traits that led him through many an adventure. The biggest of those adventures was The Greenland Expedition that located and retrieved a World War II vintage P-38 fighter plane that had been buried 265 feet beneath the ice cap for fifty years. Epps was the organizing force behind that adventure.

He had long been intrigued with the legend of the six lost P-38s awaiting rescue beneath the Greenland ice cap, and when a visiting pilot mentioned that he'd always wanted one; Epps couldn't resist the challenge. What began as a lark to locate "The Lost Squadron" of Greenland soon became his dream and his tar baby* obsession—encompassing eleven years and seven expeditions to the top of the world.

Of the six P-38s that ran out of gas in a blizzard in 1942 and were forced to land on a remote ice cap, only the "Glacier Girl" was rescued. The remaining five P-38s still lie frozen beneath the ice awaiting other visionaries.

In 1999 his peers honored Pat when he received the "American Spirit Award" from the National Business Aviation Association (NBAA). He was cited for his "courage, pursuit of excellence and service to others in the aviation community" and recognized as the organizing force behind the Greenland Expedition, his ownership of Epps Aviation and his involvement in the NBAA.

2007 marks 100 years of aviation in the state of Georgia. At Epps the future is bright and "the sky is the limit."

✧

Above: Epps Aviation founder Pat Epps (fourth from left) with his wife, Ann Hailey, by his side on the wing of his signature Aerobatic Beechcraft Bonanza with children Patrick Epps, Jr., Marian Epps Lentini and Elaine Epps Persons, who are part of the team running one of DeKalb's historic companies.

Below: Epps flies his signature red, white and blue Aerobatic Beechcraft Bonanza in local air shows.

**From Georgia's beloved author, Joel Chandler Harris,* Tales by Uncle Remus. *The parable of the tar baby is getting into something you did not plan, and getting stuck.*

HLM Financial Group

The HLM Financial Group, whose workforce and clientele are one of DeKalb's more diverse and knowledgeable, has grown in its twenty-one year history from a one-person accounting operation to one of the Atlanta metro area's most successful full-service financial institutions.

It was in 1986 when Lynn Pasqualetti, now managing partner of HLM, left a local accounting firm seeking a new challenge. She found it when she set up shop in the den of her Decatur home. Concentrating on establishing rapport with clients and meeting their needs, she saw business steadily grow. Within a couple of years, she was assembling a staff.

Laura Bevins, vice president, was the first to join the new effort in 1989. An example of the diverse backgrounds of many HLM's staff members, Laura has a Bachelor of Science degree from Bemidji University, graduated from the Georgia Law Enforcement Academy, and studied accounting at Mercer. "Over the past eighteen years, Laura has played a vital and integral role in the development of the company," Lynn said of her partner. Laura currently is working with larger firms who have "outsourced" their controller position to HLM, and she also serves as the company's accounting manager.

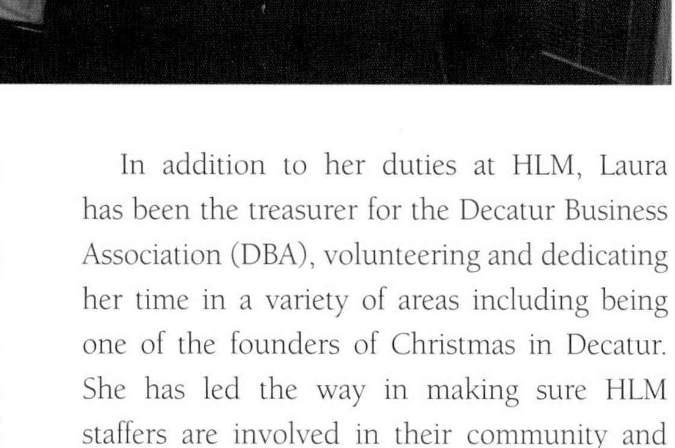

Above: Vice President Laura Bevins and President and Managing Partner Lynn Pasqualetti.

Below: Front door at office of HLM Financial Group.

In addition to her duties at HLM, Laura has been the treasurer for the Decatur Business Association (DBA), volunteering and dedicating her time in a variety of areas including being one of the founders of Christmas in Decatur. She has led the way in making sure HLM staffers are involved in their community and various nonprofit organizations.

With company growth new services were added and besides accounting, HLM now offers clients a full range of services, including management advisory services, tax preparation, representation and tax planning services, mortgages, insurance, and comprehensive financial services, including estate planning. Lynn says, "We want lifetime relationships with our clients."

"Over the years, our individual clients have become mostly upper-income taxpayers," says Lynn pointing out the needs of the upper income taxpayer is often more complex and more challenging. "Our business clientele is in the range of half-million to $25 million in annual revenues. Our average business client generates about $3 million in annual gross revenue."

Of the many services the company offers, Lynn added, "We are a one-stop financial services shop. I saw the inevitable coming when PC's came on the market and realized our business model needed to change so we started adding more services. Offering our one-stop concept has been great for our clients who have been very happy not having to go to multiple places."

Lynn who has a BS in Accounting, is an Enrolled Agent, a Certified Tax Professional from the American Institute of Tax Studies, an Accredited Tax Advisor, and is a certified graduate of the Captone Mortgage Broker Course and is the broker of record for HLM Mortgage Company. Other than accounting, her areas of expertise include taxation, consulting, business development, and as a well known speaker on the speaking circuit teaching income tax seminars and practice management to CPAs, EAs, and other tax professionals since 1992. She is also a founding director of Decatur First Bank, a member of numerous state and national professional organizations, and is on several nonprofit boards.

Mercedes Pasqualetti, President of Operations, HLM Mortgage Company, attended Agnes Scott, Georgia State, and Saddleback College in California where she studied international finance, has been with the company since 2002 and has been instrumental in developing the mortgage division. She is a certified graduate of the Capstone Mortgage Broker Course and is the company's loan specialist. "Mercedes is tenacious when it comes to finding the right product to fit the client," Lynn emphasizes.

Currently, Mercedes is on the board of the Georgia Association of Mortgage Brokers where she said, "I work to ensure all brokers and lenders meet high ethical standards."

Lawrence (Larry) Waller II, CFS, who formerly worked with Merrill-Lynch and joined HLM in 1999, is president and owner of HLM Financial Services, an arm of the HLM Financial Group. He leads a team of experienced specialists that coordinate the efforts of attorneys, tax advisors, pension managers, estate and business planners, and employee benefits coordinators working for the company's clients. "If there is some additional resource the client needs, then we pull that outside person in to help," Larry points out. "The technical term for our clients is accredited. They are investors who typically make at least $100,000 yearly and have a net worth of more than a half-million dollars."

"Larry is dedicated to providing meaningful financial solutions to individuals, professionals, and business owners on a wide range of financial matters, from risk management and investments to qualified and non-qualified retirement and benefit plans for business," Lynn commented. "His mission is to create multigenerational wealth for his clients."

"My philosophy is to pay attention to trends and move money with those trends in order to get the best returns possible, even in an uncertain market," Larry said.

HLM's modern offices have, since 2003, occupied 3500 square feet of space in the heart of downtown Decatur's Two Decatur Towncenter.

"The most exciting thing for me has been watching this company grow from just Lynn to the diverse team we have today offering a variety of services and products, not just accounting," Vice President Laura Bevins said about the company's present ten-person workforce.

Above: HLM Mortage Company President of Operations Mercedes Pasqualetti.

Below: President of HLM Financial Services, Inc., Lawrence (Larry) Waller, II.

Birthright of Atlanta

✧

Above: Available twenty-four hours a day, seven days a week, Birthright Hotline Operators respond to callers from across the country and Canada.

Below: Women find pregnancy help at the welcoming and inviting Coppage House.

Jessica was lonely and scared. She feared that her parents would kick her out of the house when they found out she was pregnant at age sixteen. They did.

Twenty-six year old Joan was at the end of her rope. She already had two children, a minimum wage job and a tiny apartment with an empty pantry. Her husband had told her that if she got pregnant again, he would leave. He did.

Every day, young girls and women like Joan and Jessica find themselves in the midst of unplanned pregnancies, alone, scared, and not knowing what to do. The good news is they do not have to be alone. There is loving and compassionate help available, and it is just a phone call away.

"We're not here to judge. We're here to provide assistance, support, and comfort to girls and women distressed by an unplanned pregnancy," said Terry Weaver, director of the Atlanta chapter and national office of Birthright International, the world's first crisis pregnancy service with nearly 400 chapters worldwide. "Rather than tell a woman, 'Don't have an abortion,' we say, 'Let us help you have your baby.'"

Like its sister chapters throughout the U.S. and abroad, Birthright of Atlanta offers loving and positive alternatives to abortion, using not only its own resources, but also resources within the community. They help their clients identify personal resources that perhaps they have yet to realize, and they provide simple, yet valuable things such as friendship and emotional support, free pregnancy testing and maternity and baby clothes. They make referrals to help their clients meet legal, medical, financial and housing needs, and provide information on prenatal development, employment searches, continuing education, adoption, pregnancy and childbirth, as well as childcare options and child safety issues.

According to Weaver, Birthright International has been in existence for nearly forty years, founded in Toronto, Ontario, Canada in 1968 by the late Louise Summerhill, a busy housewife and mother who felt something should be done to help women through an unplanned pregnancy. Birthright of Atlanta, the first of 355 chapters in the United States, followed suit the very next year, and has since become not only the home of Birthright U.S.A.'s national office, but now also hosts the organization's twenty-four-hour, year-round international hotline.

All along, a very determined, relentlessly dedicated Weaver has been at the helm, recruiting help and driving the organization forward long after most people would have given up.

"Truthfully, it hasn't always been easy, but I have never been in this alone," Weaver said, reminiscing of how she met the Birthright International founder at a pro-life meeting at a Chicago college and then came home to talk two of her best friends, Shirley Williams and Teresa Gernazian, into joining her in launching America's very first pregnancy service. "Back then, our plan was to get it all started and back off. That was thirty-eight years ago in July 2007," she added, her voice still filled with enthusiasm.

"Indeed, it has taken scores of caring people to bring us to where we are today—people like the late Dr. Mark Coppage who donated our first house in 1985 and his wife, Jean Coppage White and son Kyle, who later deeded us the house next door when they saw that we were bursting at the seams," Weaver said. "And, then there was Bill Weidmann, a gracious contractor who literally brought it all together for us. Donating his own time and utilizing the many donations made by Birthright supporters, Bill connected the two homes so that we would have enough space to operate Birthright Atlanta, the national office and international hotline."

Weaver emphasizes that Birthright is a nonprofit, tax-exempt charitable agency, fully independent and interdenominational. The organization exists solely on the financial and moral support of its donors and volunteers, and all of its services are free, confidential, and available to any woman regardless of age, race, creed, and economic or marital status. The group has never used scare tactics or pressure; has never picketed or harassed abortion clinics; has never evangelized, lobbied for legislative changes nor engaged in public debate on abortions.

Weaver added that there are two staff members and approximately forty-five volunteers operating the three busy Birthright entities located at 3424 Hardee Avenue in DeKalb County. It is estimated that 28,000 women make their first visit to a Birthright chapter worldwide every month and as many as 3,000 have utilized Birthright of Atlanta annually. Birthright's international hotline receives 64,000-plus calls per year. As to an exact number of how many babies have been saved since Birthright came into being, Weaver says no one knows for sure.

"We do know that a great many lives have been saved," Weaver said. "But, in truth, it really wouldn't matter if it had just been one. It would all still be worth it."

If you or someone you know is facing an unplanned pregnancy, feel free to call Birthright of Atlanta at 770-451-2273. You may also call the Birthright Hotline at 800-550-4900 and speak to somebody confidentially. To volunteer or become a contributor or sponsor, contact Terry Weaver at 770-451-6336.

Above: Atlanta volunteer sits with client, "making a plan."

Below: Founders of Birthright Atlanta, Shirley Williams and Terry Weaver. Birthright International founder Louise Summerhill and founder of Birthright Atlanta, Teresa Gernazian, at a luncheon in 1983.

ACE III Communications

In its short but storied seventeen-year history, *The Champion* has evolved from a publication primarily showcasing the successes of DeKalb's African-American communities to the county's newspaper of record, serving one of the most diverse populations in the nation. It is also one of the most award-winning and respected weekly newspapers in the state.

The Champion's success is a remarkable story of how a couple, through perseverance, faith, vision and hard work, took a small weekly newspaper and built a publishing company around it. Owners and publishers Carolyn and Dr. Earl Glenn began their journalistic journey in 1991—a year in which a large number of newspapers across the country folded—when he had a thriving dental practice and she was a recently retired educator raising a young son. Neither had experience in the publishing business. In her column in *The Champion*, Editor Kathy Mitchell described their quest this way: "While still pursuing their busy lives, the couple spent whatever time they could putting together the newspaper. They were the writers, designers, editors and advertising salespeople at a time when the computer did few newspaper functions. They kept up the demanding schedule, adding a small staff over time. Five years into this process, their printing representative, John Hewitt, convinced them that the newspaper had a good shot at becoming the county's legal organ. He would later become *The Champion's* general manager and is now its chief operating officer. It took an uphill battle in the courts, but in 1997 *The Champion* became the official newspaper of the state's second largest county, the largest black-owned newspaper in Georgia and one of the largest black-owned publications in the country. With its new designation, *The Champion* also had a new mission. No longer directed exclusively to the African-American community, *The Champion* started to reflect the fact that DeKalb is Georgia's most ethnically diverse county."

✧

Below: Founders Dr. Earl and Carolyn Glenn and John Hewitt, chief operating officer.

VOL. 37, NO. 36 SATURDAY, APRIL 4, 1998

Georgia Supreme Court Pens A Historic Ruling For DeKalb County's Champion Newspape[r]

BY REGINA LYNCH-HUDSON

The Champion Newspaper, an African-American owned publication, reigns triumphant in retaining its designation as the legal organ for metro Atlanta's DeKalb County, upheld by the Georgia Supreme Court. This judgement ranks *The Champion Newspaper* ...

In 2002, the first year it joined the Georgia Press Association, the paper won first place in the lifestyle, news photography, sports photography and humorous column categories in the press association's newspaper competition. The wall in the foyer of the newspaper's office is now adorned with many GPA awards, and in 2006 and 2007 *The Champion* won more awards than any other weekly newspaper in Georgia in editorial and advertising categories, including the top award for general excellence.

Becoming the legal organ for DeKalb County was an important milestone for *The Champion* and it meant that the newspaper was no longer centered exclusively on the black community. "We took on that responsibility, but at the same time we didn't want to let go of the dream that got us into the publishing business in the first place," Dr. Glenn said. In 1999, ACE III Communications, *The Champion*'s corporate parent, embarked on a new venture, *Atlanta goodlife*; a lifestyle magazine serving metro Atlanta's African-American community. "We decided to pull together a talented crew of writers, designers, photographers, and others who could make this dream happen," Dr. Glenn recalled. "We wanted to show the lifestyles of individuals who had come from different places and whose talents may or may not have been recognized." The magazine has been a success featuring celebrities and emerging achievers with strong ties to metro Atlanta.

Atlanta goodlife has also received many accolades since its inception, including ones bestowed by the Atlanta Association of Black Journalists as well as awards of excellence and best of category recognitions by the Printing Industry Association of Georgia based on overall content and design.

The history of ACE III Communications, *The Champion* and *Atlanta goodlife* is the history of key people who have helped ensure its success. Chief Operating Officer Hewitt is a jack-of-all-trades who has helped keep the publishing company on a steady course. Gale Horton Gay, managing editor of *The Champion* and editor-in-chief of *Atlanta goodlife*, and Kathy Mitchell, editor of *The Champion* and assistant editor of *Atlanta goodlife*, are veteran journalists whose talent and professionalism have helped make ACE III publications tops in their fields. At the same time, Legal Advertising Manager Jacqueline Bryant and Bookkeeper Jenese Glenn Turner operate efficient and professionally run departments, keeping pace with the legal advertising needs of a county of more than 700,000 residents.

Community service is an important part of ACE III Communications' mission, and its owners and staff are active in many civic and business organizations, including the Atlanta Business League, the DeKalb Chamber of Commerce, the South DeKalb Business Association, DeKalb Rape Crisis Center and the Atlanta Association of Black Journalists. Carolyn Glenn serves on the board of directors of Leadership DeKalb and Georgia Perimeter College. Earl Glenn serves on the boards of Partners for Community Action and the South DeKalb YMCA; and Kathy Mitchell is on the executive board of Odyssey Family Counseling Center. John Hewitt chairs the advertising committee for the Georgia Press Association and works closely with DeKalb Convention and Visitors Bureau and Leadership DeKalb.

DeKalb has a long tradition of award-winning community newspapers dating back to the 1800s. *The Champion* is the latest chapter in that proud history.

DeKalb Medical

DeKalb Medical enters a new era with a new name, but the same, unwavering mission: To improve lives through the delivery of excellent health and wellness services in partnership with physicians.

Nowhere is this mission better exemplified than in DeKalb Medical's Cancer Center. The Cancer Center's physicians, clinical professionals and volunteers are dedicated to quality, compassionate care, and utilizing innovative technology to improve the lives of cancer patients.

Breast cancer patients may receive the MammoSite Radiation Therapy System (RTS), a new technology which minimizes treatment time while preventing a recurrence of cancer. In addition, high tech genetic testing gives DeKalb Medical patients the opportunity to assess their genetic predisposition to cancer, and consider proactive treatment to prevent the deadly disease. DeKalb Medical's Treehouse Gang provides support, counseling, and education to children of cancer patients.

While continuing to strengthen its commitment to cancer treatment, DeKalb Medical is also investing in other vital clinical areas, including women's services.

The new Women's & Surgery Center at the North Decatur Road campus offers a comprehensive array of gynecological and maternity services, with an emphasis on family centered maternity care. DeKalb Medical delivers approximately 6,000 babies a year, making it one of the top five maternity programs in Georgia.

A leader in progressive medicine and patient care, DeKalb Medical has three hospital campuses, including the 451-bed DeKalb Medical at North Decatur, the 76-bed DeKalb Medical at Downtown Decatur and the 100-bed DeKalb Medical at Hillandale. The system offers the latest technologies including computer guided navigation systems used in neurosurgery, orthopedics, and ENT procedures. DeKalb Medical is home to a Bariatric Center of Excellence, as well as a certified Stroke Center. As an elite healthcare leader, DeKalb Medical is among the top five percent of hospitals nationwide to implement Computerized Physician Order Entry (CPOE), an electronic medical record system which reduces the possibility of medical errors due to illegible handwriting.

DeKalb Medical employs more than 3,800 medical, nursing and support staff members and has approximately 775 physicians. Each year, more than 400 volunteers complement the staff by donating nearly 64,000 hours of their time and talents. DeKalb Medical offers comprehensive health and wellness services throughout the region, handling more than 24,000 hospital admissions, 113,000 emergency room visits, and 292,000 outpatient visits in the average year. This marks astonishing growth from DeKalb Medical's inception nearly fifty years ago.

The DeKalb Hospital Authority was created in 1957 after voters approved a hospital bond referendum which was matched by federal funds. The North Decatur Road site was then purchased for $160,000 and William H. Thrasher, one of the few people in the South with a master's degree in hospital administration was chosen as its first administrator. After three years of planning, advocacy, and determination, Thrasher guided the new facility from blueprint to ribbon cutting. In 1961, DeKalb General Hospital opened its doors.

Thrasher explained his goal for the new hospital, a goal which still applies today: "Personnel have been instructed and recruited on a theory designed to eliminate many of the complaints often heard about hospitals. They will look at their duties in their relationship with the patient as if they, themselves, were the patient."

Together, with a sixty-six member medical staff, Thrasher and the hospital's 300 employees

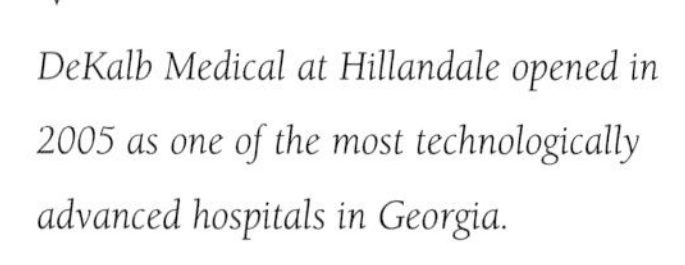

DeKalb Medical at Hillandale opened in 2005 as one of the most technologically advanced hospitals in Georgia.

began their work, "Dedicated to the Glory of God and to the Improved Health of Mankind," as proclaimed by a plaque in the lobby.

That message resonated through nearly five decades, as DeKalb General Hospital became DeKalb Medical Center in 1989, and then evolved to become DeKalb Medical in 2007.

In 2005, DeKalb Medical opened its new hospital at the Hillandale campus, culminating a more than three decade push by DeKalb Medical to expand healthcare access for south DeKalb residents. The effort began in 1970, when DeKalb County voters first approved a $1.95 million bond referendum to help fund a south DeKalb hospital. For thirty-five years, DeKalb Medical kept alive the community's dreams, acquiring the Hillandale site in Lithonia, navigating through many rounds of legal opinions and feasibility studies, and working for state approval to open a hospital serving south DeKalb.

Finally, the dream became a reality, and DeKalb Medical at Hillandale opened as Georgia's first master planned all-digital hospital.

According to DeKalb Medical President and Chief Executive Officer Eric Norwood, the success of the new Hillandale campus, and the growth of the North Decatur and Downtown Decatur campuses reflect a renaissance in the community. Norwood says DeKalb Medical is Pushing Beyond traditional expectations in healthcare.

"We have grown and developed new services in so many ways that we are reintroducing ourselves to our community. When we talk about Pushing Beyond, we believe that this is just descriptive of a new attitude at DeKalb Medical in recent years that says we are always looking to improve on the status quo. We are embracing positive change, bringing new technology and new innovations to the way that we care for patients," said Norwood.

Above: The new Women's & Surgery Center is located at 2701 North Decatur Road.

Below: Craftman style interiors with special textures, colors and details are blended together to provide an environment that is calming to patients as well as visitors.

Steel, Inc.

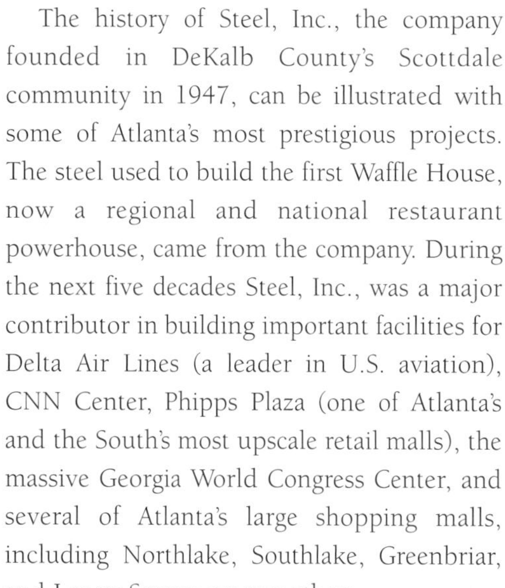

The history of Steel, Inc., the company founded in DeKalb County's Scottdale community in 1947, can be illustrated with some of Atlanta's most prestigious projects. The steel used to build the first Waffle House, now a regional and national restaurant powerhouse, came from the company. During the next five decades Steel, Inc., was a major contributor in building important facilities for Delta Air Lines (a leader in U.S. aviation), CNN Center, Phipps Plaza (one of Atlanta's and the South's most upscale retail malls), the massive Georgia World Congress Center, and several of Atlanta's large shopping malls, including Northlake, Southlake, Greenbriar, and Lenox Square among others.

Celebrating its sixtieth anniversary in 2007, the company was begun by Karl Kranig as a subsidiary of Bristol (Virginia) Steel. In 1963 he bought out the parent company becoming sole owner and named Atlanta native Gene Holloway as the company's vice president. Holloway began his career with the company in the early 1950s, working his way through the ranks in various jobs until being named president in 1971. He guided the company for the next thirty years during some of its most productive and profitable years. "It was during his leadership that our company took a quantum leap," current President Skip Burdette said. "He was not only a mentor to me but to many others in the company as well."

✧

Above: Steel, Inc. furnished the structure and was the fabricator for one of the tallest airport control towers in the nation at Atlanta Hartsfield International Airport, the world's busiest.

Below: These heavy transfer trusses, installed by Steel, Inc. to help support The Mansion on Peachtree Street across from Lenox Mall, are among the many steel structures fabricated and installed by the company.

Kranig's experience as a salesman with Bristol Steel gave him the experience in the iron and steel industries to envision the potential for its expansion in the Southeast immediately after WWII. With attention to detail, close ties to local contractors, and a dedicated workforce noted for its longevity with the company, Steel, Inc. grew from a medium size structural steel fabricator to a major player in steel construction in Atlanta and the Southeast, developing the well-deserved reputation it has today for service and quality.

In 1986 when Kranig, by then an octogenarian, decided to sell the company, Holloway put together a group of key long-time employees that includes Jim Newton, Skip Burdette, and Dan Williams, for a highly leveraged buyout. After the buyout, the company continued to move forward using its same formula of service and quality to expand the business. In 1997 the new ownership reached a milestone when the buyout debt was retired. During the 1990s, Steel, Inc., enjoyed unparalleled success and growth which has continued into the next decade.

Burdette, who began work with the company when he was eighteen, epitomizes the blue collar work ethic that drives Steel, Inc. An article in the *Atlanta-Journal Constitution* described his ascent in the company this way: "He worked his way literally from scrap heap to the top. He began as a blueprint boy, or apprentice draftsman, but also worked in the shop, mostly in the paint area. He later moved into the sales department and eventually became the company's sole owner and third president."

In 2000, Steel, Inc., joined the Fabrications Technologies consortium, which was dissolved in 2004 and was replaced by Fab South LLC, which includes the four strongest operating companies from the original consortium. The company's name was then changed to Steel, LLC.

Over the years, Steel, Inc., has continued to fine tune its organization in order to develop and strengthen its manufacturing as well as its project management capabilities. Many specialties have resulted, ranging from conventional steel structures to complex steel building structures: commercial office buildings (low to high rise), mid-rise office campuses, distribution centers, pedestrian bridges, regional shopping malls, libraries, hotels, sports arenas, convention centers, parking decks, pulp and paper mills, chemical plants, communication and manufacturing plants, automobile assembly plants, metal refining plants, power plants, cargo facilities, airline hubs, terminals and concourses, airline baggage handling facilities, airport transit system structures, airline maintenance and paint hangers, airport control towers and airplane test jigs, stands and tanks.

"...Whether we're fabricating structural steel for an office building or for a jumbo jet paint hanger, our goal is simple: give contractors, construction managers, and owners structural steel that insures the success of each project and endures for decades to come, and structural steel that lives up to our name. . . "

In a recent message to new employees of Steel, Inc., Burdette summed up the firm's history and mission. "...You are joining a proud organization which has been in business at this same location since 1947. Steel, Inc., is a leader in structural steel fabrication in the Southeast, providing our customers with service that is unsurpassed in our industry. Customer satisfaction is a hallmark of Steel, Inc., where over seventy-five percent of work is performed for repeat customers. This is true due to the dedication of our employees and the pride they take in their work."

And he added, "The continued growth of Steel, Inc., into the next millennium will bring new challenges and opportunities. It is this type of challenge that will continue to allow Steel, Inc., to grow and continue to be part of the future progress of Georgia and the Southeast."

✧

Above: Celebrating the company's sixtieth anniversary in 2007, Steel, Inc.'s dedicated work force gathers in front of the firm's mammoth, modern steel fabrication plant in DeKalb's Scottdale community.

Below: Steel, Inc.'s specialty steel handiwork is on display in the popular and unique Pulse Bar in Atlanta's largest hotel, the Marriott Marquis

Decatur First Bank

Above: The Decatur First Bank Board of Directors. Front row (from left to right): John Walter Drake, Dr. Bobbie Bailey, Robert E. Lanier, Judy B. Turner, Lynn Pasqualetti and James A. Baskett. Back row: James T. Smith, III, Kirby A. Thompson, William F. Floyd, John L. Adams, Jr., Director Emeritus Merriell Autrey, Jr., Roger K. Quillen, and Carol G. Nickola.

Below: The main office of Decatur First Bank at 1120 Commerce Drive in Decatur.

In 2007 Decatur First Bank celebrated its first decade as a full service financial institution serving not only DeKalb County, but also with a Lake Oconee division with offices in Greensboro, Madison, and Athens.

Decatur First Bank opened in September of 1997 when a group of key business and professional DeKalb Countians determined there was a need for a bank to serve the community after the consolidation of some local financial institutions. Decatur First is fulfilling its goal to support and improve the communities it serves.

Among the key individuals who were founders in the early days and who still serve the community in various civic and business roles were John L. Adams, Jr., Merriell Autrey, Jr., James A. Baskett, Mary Bobbie Bailey, John Walter Drake, William F. Floyd, Robert E. Lanier, Carol G. Nickola, Lynn Pasqualetti, Roger K. Quillen, James T. Smith, III, Kirby A. Thompson, and Judy B. Turner, president of the bank.

Decatur First is dedicated to the needs of the residents and businesses it serves. All decisions are made locally and funds reinvested in the community. "Our goal is to build long-lasting relationships and improve the lives and livelihoods of our shareholders, the customers we serve, and our employees, while actively supporting our community," Turner commented. Besides Turner, senior management includes Executive Vice President Ann Randall and Executive Vice President/Senior Lender Gregory M. Autrey.

Turner relates, "how it all started," when what is now Bank of America announced it was buying Bank South, a group of community people got together and discussed the need for a local bank to fill a void.

"The community had already lost two of its major corporate citizens, Decatur Federal Savings and Loan and Citizens and Southern National Bank. Some banking consultants saw an opportunity to assist a local group in starting a new bank," Turner explained. "They contacted me and discussed what would need to be done to make it happen."

Turner, a long time veteran in the banking business, and the consultants discussed the need to find eight to ten people who would commit to serving on the board of directors. Those individuals were required to purchase a minimum of $100,000 of stock, advance $5000 for organization expenses and talk with others about buying stock as well as using their time and expertise to oversee the organization of the bank.

The late Jack Dunn, a prominent DeKalb banker who was the Georgia Commissioner of Banking at the time Decatur First was being organized, was a strong supporter of the bank. "Because of his belief in us, we received our charter less than a month after we submitted our application to the State Department of Banking and Finance," Turner pointed out.

Commenting on Turner's role with the bank, founding director Walter Drake said, "Throughout her banking career prior to the formation of Decatur First Bank, Turner personified the 'community volunteer.' It was quite logical that she would organize a true community bank, which actively participates in the community and encourages a culture of civic involvement among its staff and employees."

Decatur First has come a long way since it was organized in a cramped former dental office. Today, the modern headquarters on Commerce Drive in Decatur houses the main office. In 2000 residents of Clairmont Place Senior Living Community requested the bank open an office there. Other DeKalb locations are in the Commerce Drive Kroger store and the Panola Road office located on Fairington Road in Lithonia.

At its inception the bank was required to raise $8 million by selling stock at $10 per share. Decatur First actually raised nearly $10 million with a million and a half being raised the last day the bank was accepting subscriptions to buy stock.

Striving to attract as many local investors as possible in the early days, Decatur First accepted subscriptions of one $10 share. "This allowed many younger local people who really wanted to be part of the bank to invest," Turner said.

There were long hours as employees worked twenty-three hours straight to meet the bank's opening date. Those long hours have paid off, and today Decatur First ranks among the top local banks in metro Atlanta with assets exceeding $180 million.

Among the prominent community organizations with which both officers of the bank and directors are involved include the DeKalb Historical Society, Decatur Education Foundation, South Decatur Community Development Corporation, DeKalb Council for the Arts, Decatur Book Festival, Housing Authority of DeKalb County, Columbia Theological Seminary, Agnes Scott College, and Wesley Woods.

"The bank is dedicated to continuing to support the communities in which we do business," Turner emphasizes. "We are adding products that are needed in these communities to be responsive to the needs of our customers."

Above: The lobby of Decatur First Bank is home to a beautiful eggshell mosaic mural by noted artist Athos Menaboni.

Below: (From left to right) Ben Berg, Doris Shelton, and Pam Bradley. The popcorn is always hot and delicious at Decatur First Bank.

Organization of DeKalb Educators

"I believe the children are our future. Teach them well and let them lead the way." While these are the opening lyrics to Whitney Houston's 1985 chart-topping hit, "Greatest Love of All," they could just as easily be the theme for the Organization of DeKalb Educators—a group that understands the importance of a great public education and strives to provide the county they serve with the best education system possible.

Often referred to by its acronym, ODE, the Organization of DeKalb Educators was founded in 1974 and is the local affiliate of the Georgia Association of Educators and the National Education Association. It is a vibrant, dynamic school and community-based professional organization dedicated to improving education in the DeKalb County School System as well as the overall quality of life for all of DeKalb County. Its mission is to be the leader in providing information, training, representation and support for teachers, education support personnel, students and parents alike.

Today, ODE represents almost 5,000 DeKalb County School System employees and is the largest local professional education affiliate in Georgia.

"We are, in essence, the leading voice of our county's public educators," said ODE President David Schutten. "Because we wholeheartedly believe that an education system is only as good as its educators, we continuously lobby for improved teaching and learning conditions, and work hard to support, shield and strengthen those who foster DeKalb County's most precious resource: its children."

Though enormously successful today, the road has not always been smooth. In fact, the organization's birth was actually the result of a struggle that started over a 1968 report critical of the DeKalb school system and published by the National Education Association (NEA). Upset over the report, school administrators put intense pressure on the county's then only association of educators—the DeKalb Association of Educators—to sever its affiliation with NEA as well as its state affiliation with the Georgia Association of Educators (GAE). When the DeKalb association did cut its ties, both NEA and GAE took immediate action to organize a new local affiliate and ODE was born.

Pioneer organizers of ODE included DeKalb educators William Driskell, Edith Nash, Jerry Minear, Anne Wilson, Geraldine Pearson, Dawn Hamer, Gwendolyn Drayne, Betty Leslein, and Martha Parker. Many others, just as dedicated, joined along the way.

At first, the new group was not welcomed at all by school system administrators. Simple requests were denied and cooperation was virtually nonexistent. There were periods, in fact, that the organization was able to do little more than survive and membership dwindled significantly.

And, yet, they never gave up. ODE's members—as few as they may have been—were determined to keep the torch burning, and that determination finally began to pay off in the late

1980s and early 1990s. It was during this time that a new group of educators, all of whom possessed experience with the National Education Association, transferred into the DeKalb County school system. Immediately stepping up to the plate to help revitalize ODE and its lobbying efforts at both the local and state levels were newcomers Jackie Henry, Johnese Threadcraft, Gloria Slaughter, Bill Gruber, Rosilind Taylor and David Schutten.

In addition to the infusion of new leadership, membership also received a boost about the same time. After ODE Treasurer Helen Zappia retired from her normal teaching job, she used her new found time to increase communication with and service to ODE members. Under the leadership of GAE Uniserv Director Pete Toggerson, she joined forces with then President Rosilind Taylor to develop a new membership plan that yielded dynamic membership growth. Communication and collaboration with school system administrators also improved dramatically and ODE cemented its role as "the leading voice for public education in DeKalb County."

Over the years, ODE has helped to pass SPLOSTs to pay for school system improvements; has lobbied for pay raises and other needs of school system employees; has established and co-administered scholarship programs such as the Levi A. Simon III Scholarship; and has worked side-by-side with other local groups such as DeKalb County's Family Support Center, the Southern Order of Storytellers, and Atlantans Building Leadership for Empowerment, a multiracial community organization focused on improving schools, neighborhood services, housing opportunities and jobs programs.

In 2000, ODE began adopting schools in the county. ODE has adopted fifteen schools, providing them with additional resources and support. A true milestone occurred in the relationship between ODE and the DeKalb County School System when ODE became a system-wide Partner in Education in March 2007 at the DeKalb Chamber of Commerce monthly lunch. Now ODE is a collaborative formal partner with the school system, working together to achieve excellence in the school system.

Additionally, ODE has been aggressive in securing state and national grants to help fund and sponsor numerous community projects such as Read With Me DeKalb, Read Across America, the Helen Ruffin Reading Bowl, and the PeachSeed Storytelling Festival and Conference for Young Tellers, all events designed to reach out to the community and promote literacy and educational activities.

The organization is also a member of the Teacher Union Reform Network, an influential nationwide network committed to education reform and raising student achievement.

For more information on the Organization of DeKalb Educators, visit www.odegaenea.org or call 678-837-1170.

Centers for Disease Control & Prevention

"In northeast Atlanta, in buildings of sturdy but unprepossessing appearance, is an extraordinary institution, the Centers for Disease Control and Prevention." This was written back in 1992 in Elizabeth Etheridge's preface to her book, *Sentinel for Health: A History of the Centers for Disease Control*. In the fifteen years since, CDC remains an extraordinary institution, but today its Atlanta campus is as impressive as the work done within its walls.

Growing from a small unit of the U.S. Public Health Service (USPHS) assigned to fight malaria in the south, CDC began its journey in Atlanta, Georgia, in the early 1940s. Known then as Malaria Control in War Areas, CDC soon was called on to broaden its activities in scope and reach, to as far away as California, investigating, fighting, and controlling other diseases, such as dengue fever and murine typhus.

In 1946 this unit of the USPHS found a permanent home in DeKalb County on land donated by Emory University. Its name was changed as well to the Communicable Disease Center to more aptly describe the broad work that this institution would be undertaking in disease control.

Under the direction of its first director, Dr. Joseph Mountin, CDC provided service for a variety of public health concerns, including environmental concerns, emerging health problems, and communicable diseases. CDC provided assistance to all states and gave science and research a practical application that would help to meet the health needs throughout the country at that time and continues to do so today.

From its headquarters in Atlanta to places across the country and the world, CDC has had many milestones over its sixty-one years. In 1949, CDC declared the United States free

of malaria as a significant health problem; in the 1960s, after a decade of research and surveillance, declared the eradication of smallpox in the United States; in the 1970s, the eradication of polio; in the 1980s, made the first diagnosis of the fatal disease AIDS and began the ongoing battle to fight this disease in this country and around the world; and in 2006, CDC declared the elimination of rubella in the United States. These milestones are impressive, but only touch the surface of the tremendous work done by world-class doctors, scientists, and epidemiologists.

The number of employees at CDC and the Agency for Toxic Substances and Disease Registrys (ATSDR; CDC's sister agency) totals more than 14,000 in 40 countries and in 170 occupations with a public health focus, including physicians, statisticians, epidemiologists, laboratory experts, behavioral scientists, and health communicators. CDC/ATSDR is the only federal agency located outside of Washington, D.C., and it ranks twenty-second among Georgia's top employers, with approximately two-thirds of its employees here at the headquarters location.

Currently, CDC locations in DeKalb County total six, from the headquarters location on Clifton Road, to Chamblee, North Druid Hills, Buford Highway, Lawrenceville, and Decatur. The Atlanta locations provide this institution with a perspective that keeps its focus not only on scientific excellence but also on the missionary spirit that is CDC—to protect the health of all people. CDC keeps humanity at the forefront of its mission of Healthy People in a Healthy World. They may be the world's premier public health agency, but their work and their success begin with that one person that is reached with lifesaving information and tools. With CDC, Healthy People in a Healthy World begins right here at home in DeKalb County and Atlanta.

A. S. TURNER & SONS, INC.

Born in the horse and buggy era in the early 1900's as a hardware store which sold caskets, DeKalb's A. S. Turner & Sons Funeral Home is today one of the state's and the nation's premier institutions of its kind with a tradition of ninety-four years of caring community service.

A. S. Turner & Sons has a varied and rich history. Its founder Addison Stewart Turner was born in the late 1800's in nearby Rockdale County, the son of a prominent farmer and minister. A family history recounts how. "Mr. Turner sold sewing machines for a while and in 1903 was financially able to form a partnership of Turner and Johnson, mainly a hardware store that sold caskets in Conyers . . . Many farmers would drive their wagon into town, purchase a casket and go back to the farm to have a 'do it yourself at home' funeral."

In 1917, Addison became the sole owner of the funeral home and his teenage son, A. Mell Turner, became active in the business, leaving briefly to serve in the Army in World War I. Carlton, the second Turner son, joined the business in the late twenties and by 1936 the business had outgrown its North McDonough location. That year A. S. Turner purchased the former home of Holy Episcopal Church at the corner of Trinity and Church Streets and had the sanctuary remodeled for a chapel and built staterooms, offices and a showroom. It opened the first day of 1938.

Above: Spacious state-of-the-art home of A. S. Turner & Sons today on North Decatur Road adjacent to DeKalb Medical Center.

Below: Portaits of sons, Mell and Carlton flank their father's, founder A. S. Turner in the North Decatur facility.

Unfortunately, Addison died later that year from a brain tumor, and Mell and Carlton now operated the firm, which had grown to five employees and included Ann Shealy, who was with the firm for sixty years until her retirement in 1998.

In 1959, Turner's moved from the old Episcopal Church on Trinity Place, which it had turned into a modern mortuary facility, to the spacious state-of-the art facility it now occupies on North Decatur Road adjacent to the DeKalb Medical Center.

The history of A. S. Turner & Sons is one of a dedicated family, which mirrors the progress of Decatur and DeKalb. Mell became known as one of DeKalb's early business and civic leaders.

When a third son, Ralph, joined the firm, A. S. Turner was now truly a family affair. When Carlton and Ralph entered the service during World War II, Mell ran the business until they returned in 1945.

Carlton died in 1968 and Mell died in 1977, leaving Ralph as the new chief operating officer. In 1972, Ralph's son Fred joined the firm and is now chief operating officer. In 1996, Ralph's daughter Jane came aboard and is now active in the firm after serving several years in the Peace Corps.

Today A. S. Turner and Sons is one of the largest family-owned funeral homes in the state and nation with a staff offering more than 500 years of professional experience to serve the public.

The firm has ties to thousands of quality funeral homes in the United States, which enables it to extend services out of town. Its highly professional staff keeps up-to-date by regularly participating in training and development programs nationwide. Most importantly, the staff is trained to

provide ways for families and friends to participate in the service, which helps in the healing process.

A. S. Turner & Sons is prepared to assist families on a daily round-the-clock basis, offering one of the best and most complete selections of funeral and cremation services and products in the metro area and the state.

Another important Turner feature is providing its multiple services to people of diverse faiths and cultural roots. The firm also provides a safe and secure advanced planning program.

As part of Turner's community commitment, it provides a variety of community services, including Holiday Memorial Services, hospice activities, professional speakers on topics concerning death, grief and bereavement, support groups, specialized seminars and workshops for allied professions, and tours and education opportunities for schools, universities, colleges and churches.

A. S. Turner & Sons has a unique service designed to learn from families, which encourages input through questionnaires, letters, phone calls, e-mails and personal visits following services.

"We strive daily to create meaningful relationships with people. We are not just about business," Fred Turner said. "Our firm is committed to the long-term vision of service to our community."

Its spacious facility on North Decatur Road has more than adequate ability to serve any family's needs. Emphasizing the high level of family satisfaction over the years, Turner has hundreds of testimonial letters on hand.

"At A. S. Turner & Sons we strive to do whatever it takes to serve the needs of those who call us," Fred emphasizes. "Our purpose is to assist families with a difficult reality of life's most stressful transitions. We are committed to bringing the realities of a loved one's death and the commemoration of their life into a healing crossroads—a life mark in which family and friends can refer to their experience as a healing one."

For additional information on the services available to you from A. S. Turner & Sons, Inc., visit www.asturner.com on the Internet.

Below: Patriarch Ralph Turner took over as head of the funeral home in 1977 after the deaths of his brothers, Carlton and Mell, and was later joined by son, Fred, now chief operating officer, and daughter Jane.

Pete Garcia Company, Inc.

It was 1956 when nineteen year-old Pete Garcia began his career in the wholesale florist business driving a delivery truck in Jacksonville, Florida. In the late 1950s, Pete quickly worked his way from truck driver to manager and had served in several positions with the Oscar G. Carlstedt Co. Wholesale Florist when, in the early 1960s, he was sent to manage a store in West Palm Beach, Florida. Later he went to work as one of the nation's top floral manufacturer's representatives. After traveling throughout the country and Canada building the business and a formidable sales force, the Pete Garcia Company began operation in 1967 and was incorporated four years later. In 1973 the firm opened offices on DeKalb's Memorial Drive and when business quadrupled in 1975, the move was made to a new 20,000-square-foot building on Peachtree Industrial Boulevard in Chamblee. The company headquarters has been expanded to 45,000 square feet with elegant, dark paneled, well appointed offices on the first floor and an expansive 30,000-square-foot showroom, FloraMart®, on the ground floor. Today, as founder and principal owner of Pete Garcia Company, Garcia Group, Inc., and its many subsidiaries, Pete and his extended family run the largest supplier of floral hard goods in North America.

Another outgrowth of the company came in 1991 when Pete helped formulate Flora-Stats under the aegis of the American Floral Endowment.

The history of the Pete Garcia Company is one of a family business driven with a passion for excellence. "Efficiency, consideration, and loyalty—that's the Pete Garcia Company," Pete exclaims. His younger brother Ramon, who has been involved in the company prior to its incorporation in 1971, sums up Pete's role this way: "Pete is the ultimate coach. There is one word that really summarizes this company, and it is passion. He has the passion and the insight that drives the company."

The legacy of the Garcia family dating back to Spain and patriarch Joseph A. Garcia, Sr., who immigrated to this country in the early 1900s, is at the heart and soul of the company. The entire family, including Pete's wife Brenda, children David and Kathy, play vital roles. Son Mike Garcia was a major influence in the company until his untimely death in 1992. After retiring from a forty-three year career with the railroad, father Joe Garcia came to work when he was in his eighties and contributed his skills in woodworking to company projects until in his early nineties.

Every six months (May and November) the FloraMart® showroom undergoes a metamorphosis when the entire staff and personnel brought in from the outside join to prepare FloraMart®. "It is a time when creativity, teamwork and pride come together to create the excitement that is FloraMart®", Pete points out. "Everyone in the company joins in this endeavor," Pete emphasizes, "every level employee, including spouses." Customers from all over North America come to purchase the latest wares offered by the company. This signals the beginning of the most intensive sales. Designers come in to arrange themes for the next season. Over 65,000 items including

✧

Above: Plus One Imports Blue Green Christmas Collection at Floramart®.

Below: Front Row: Brenda B. Garcia, Beverly Garcia, Kathy Headlee and Brenda S. Garcia. Back Row: Ramon Garcia, David Garcia, Jim Headlee, Johnny Childers and Pete Garcia.

candles, flowers, ribbons, and containers are coordinated and distributors are invited to give feedback and suggestions.

With Dave as president of Pete Garcia Company and Garcia Group, Inc., business continues to grow at a steady pace as the company focuses on maximizing the benefits to its growing number of customers throughout North America, the Caribbean, and Latin America. Dave has assembled a youthful team that will continue to serve the floral industry.

Team effort is the hallmark of the Garcia Company, and its employees are part of an extended family, which has contributed to the company's success. In the early days among those making major contributions besides Pete and Ramon, were Brenda S. Garcia, Pete's wife, Brenda B. Garcia, Ramon's wife, Mike Garcia, David Garcia, Hop Hopkins, B. J. Hodges, Evelyn Porchak, Attorney Dale Dewberry, CPA Bob Bradshaw, and the invaluable support of Mom and Dad Garcia.

The Garcia companies are active in both community and floral industry affairs. Since the early 1980s an affiliation with the North DeKalb Training Center for the Handicapped has been one of the company's groundbreaking community projects. The Garcia family has for many years held leadership roles in Floral Industry Associations. Pete was president of the Wholesale Florists & Florist Suppliers Association 1979-1980. David currently holds that same office. Prior to their terms as president, they both served on the board of directors and numerous committees within the organization. Ramon served on the board of directors of the Society of American Florists and later became treasurer. Pete served for many years, in numerous capacities, on the American Floral Endowment. He later became chairman.

It is clear that the Garcia family likes to "give back."

✧

Above: David, Beverly and Mike Garcia.

Below: Plus One Imports Traditional Christmas Collection at Floramart®.

EMORY UNIVERSITY

Emory University is an internationally renowned institution of higher education, research and healthcare, whose roots trace to 1836. In that year a small college named for a recently deceased Bishop, John Emory, was founded in a Georgia hamlet dubbed Oxford, by an idealistic group of Methodists who wanted their new academy to mold character as well as mind. By 1919 the rapidly growing institution had moved nearly forty miles west to its current location in the Druid Hills area of DeKalb County.

Today, Emory numbers more than 12,500 undergraduate, graduate and professional students, and includes nine undergraduate and graduate divisions as well as the state's largest and most comprehensive system of healthcare. But it maintains a lifeline to its birthplace in the form of a highly-competitive two-year school of liberal arts called Oxford College, whose students commute to activities on the main campus in Internet-equipped shuttle buses.

Emory is enriched by the legacy and energy of Atlanta, whose downtown is just fifteen minutes away. Through collaboration among its schools, units, and centers, as well as with affiliated institutions such as The Carter Center and the U.S. Centers for Disease Control and Prevention, Emory is committed to working for positive transformation in the world.

The University's master plan outlines a bold vision for sustainable development on its 700-acre campus, which consists of fifty-four percent protected forest despite its proximity to the largest city in the Southeast. The University boasts more square feet of LEED-certified "green" building space than any other campus in America and maintains a large and growing stake in alternatively fueled shuttle buses, the use of local and sustainable food sources, and the recycling of waste products. In recognition of its many connections to the community, Emory was one of sixty schools in the U.S. recognized as an "Engaged Institution" by the Carnegie Foundation for the Advancement of Teaching.

Below: Promises to keep: Compassion, imagination, discovery, translation, caring, courage, and hope are etched in this massive stone staircase located in the Winship Cancer Institute Building.

Emory maintains an uncommon balance: it generates more sponsored-research funding than any other university in Georgia, while maintaining a rich tradition of outstanding teaching. In recent years, acclaimed novelist Salman Rushdie and His Holiness the XIV Dalai Lama joined faculty ranks that already included former U.S. President Jimmy Carter.

Perennially ranked among the top twenty national universities by *U. S. News & World Report,* Emory was one of twenty-five top schools tapped as a "New Ivy" in *Kaplan/Newsweek's 2007* "How to Get into College Guide," and was judged eighth in the country for best value among private universities in the 2007 *Kiplinger's Personal Finance Magazine.*

Emory's colleges and schools include (in addition to Oxford) Emory College, a four-year undergraduate school of liberal arts; the Candler School of Theology; the Goizueta Business School; the Emory Law School; and three nationally ranked schools comprising the Woodruff Health Sciences Center—the

School of Medicine, the Rollins School of Public Health, and the Nell Hodgson Woodruff School of Nursing.

Also included in the health sciences center are the Yerkes National Primate Research Center, the Emory Clinic, and the Emory Hospitals—Emory University Hospital and Wesley Woods Center on Clifton Road, as well as Emory Crawford Long Hospital in Midtown and several other affiliated facilities. Many Atlantans and Georgians know Emory best through its healthcare programs, among them the Emory Heart Center and the Winship Cancer Institute. Emory Healthcare logs more than 53,000 hospital admissions and 2.4 million outpatient visits every year.

Emory benefits from having a student body that is the most ethnically and religiously diverse of any of the top twenty national research universities. Emory houses a chapter of Phi Beta Kappa, the oldest and most prestigious academic honor society, and Emory students have received Rhodes, Marshall, Fulbright, Goldwater, Rotary, Rockefeller, Mellon, and *USA Today* scholarships as well as National Science Foundation Fellowships.

The University's economic impact on DeKalb County and the entire region is profound. Emory is the largest private employer in metro Atlanta, with more than 21,000 employees, including approximately 3,200 faculty members. Emory received $354 million in sponsored research in 2006, and, according to a recent study commissioned by the University, spends more than $2.6 billion in the metro area each year for a total estimated impact on the economy of $5.7 billion.

In addition to their excellence in scholarship, Emory's students shine in music, the arts and athletics, exhibiting multifaceted talents and attracting tens of thousands of visitors onto campus each year for sporting contests and artistic exhibitions and performances.

Emory fields eighteen varsity teams under the auspices of NCAA Division III, whose member schools do not award athletic scholarships. As testimony to the careful balance it maintains between games and classroom, Emory has had more student-athletes receive NCAA Postgraduate Scholarships than any other NCAA school in the past four years.

At the same time, the University's arts programs bring together 200,000 students, faculty, guest artists, and visitors each year in a spirit of collaboration and discovery. Major draws are the Michael C. Carlos Museum and the Schwartz Center for Performing Arts. Offerings include music, theater, and dance performances, art exhibitions, poetry readings, and film screenings.

Additional information on Emory University is available on the Internet at www.emory.edu.

Serdi

When Serdi, which leads the field in providing a complete range of state-of-the-art cylinder head machine systems for the world, decided to move into the U.S. market two decades ago it chose Atlanta's DeKalb County.

The company's office at 1526 Litton Drive in the Stone Mountain Industrial Park in the heart of DeKalb, which opened in 1986, serves both the North and South American markets.

"Atlanta was the best place for us for many reasons, and DeKalb County was the best place in the metro area for us," said Michael Echenoz, Serdi vice president, who moved here five years ago from his native France to run the French firm's affiliate, which serves not only the U.S. market but also Canada, Mexico, and all of Central and South America. He cites Atlanta's airport and the quality of life in the city and DeKalb County as major reasons for choosing the area. "It's only a six hour time lag from here to France," he pointed out.

The company which is based in the scenic city of Annecy, France, was founded in the early 1970s and since that time has become the worldwide leader in its field.

Although Serdi's products are highly popular in high performance vehicle circles, such as NASCAR, its application is universal, serving engines of all kinds, shapes, and sizes.

As an example, Echenoz says when Serdi began selling in the U.S. in the late 1980s, "We would travel all over the country with trucks displaying our Serdi machine, and it was like selling ice cream because our product was so new and innovative that everyone wanted one."

The list for applications of Serdi machines is eclectic and seemingly endless, including all types of motor cars, high performance racing engines, motorcycle engines, marine engines, Diesel truck engines, locomotive engines, stationary engines, small engines, and any other kind you can name.

✧

Above: Displays in the Serdi manufacturing headquarters in Annecy, France.

Recognized worldwide among engine remanufacturers and manufacturers as the unchallenged leader in valve seat machining, Serdi offers a selection of competitive technological products covering all areas of cylinder head repair and remanufacturing.

Since beginning operation in this hemisphere, Serdi has sold thousands of machines in the U.S. alone. The high precision product usually sells for from $25,000 to $125,000.

Ubiquitous Serdi products are particularly sought after by those in the auto racing business. "We had NASCAR early on, and now we have all kinds of other racing circuits for high performance cars wanting our products," Echenoz points out.

Commenting on those who utilize Serdi machines Echenoz says, "In the U.S. it's mainly about the performance industry and Diesel O.E.M, but in other countries it's more about refurbishing engines." As an example, in countries like Argentina more than fifty percent of machines are sold to repair shops.

Many individuals will purchase Serdi machines for their garages. "We have one guy in Canada who purchased a machine for his garage because it's like a hobby for him," Echenoz related.

One of the big strengths of the Serdi machine is that an individual unschooled in the intricacies of engines can be trained in a short time to use it. "If you have no clue about the machine," Echenoz explains, "it will take less than a week to learn how to use it."

Among Serdi's numerous list of patents is the "unique multiple plane air float centering system" which is acclaimed for ultimate precision, flexibility, and user friendliness.

Serdi's worldwide dominance of its field is reflected in a list of customers which include major U.S. firms such as G.M., Ford, Chrysler, and Caterpillar and top of the line foreign firms like Peugeot, Mercedes, Volkswagen, Lamborghini, and Ferrari.

Despite increasing oil prices and technology changes such as hybrid vehicles, Echenoz sees a bright future for Serdi in this country and elsewhere. The company recently renewed the lease for its Stone Mountain office.

✧

Above: The versatile Serdi seat and guide machine (4.0 power) used by top performance shops and major firms such as Daimler, Chrysler and Ford. As well as major repair shops like A.E.R., Jasper and Caterpillar.

Below: Serdi's signature V8 Block MOPAR NASCAR cylinder head.

DeKalb Technical College

✧

Above: DeKalb Technical College, Clarkson Campus, c. 1960. The original architectural rendering.

Below: The new world-class Conference Center provides for DeKalb Technical College a viable link with the community.

From its 1961 inaugural class of eighteen students studying simple electronics to today's student body of nearly 20,000 working towards degrees, diplomas and certificates in many fields of study, DeKalb Technical College (DTC) has certainly come a long way.

Indeed, DTC is dedicated to providing real-world skills for rewarding careers, and in fiscal year 2007, served 18,420 students and conferred 1,608 awards to graduates. Students throughout metro-Atlanta attend DeKalb Tech and represent all age and socio-economic brackets. Graduates have a most-impressive 99 percent job placement rate with 90.2 percent graduate placement in jobs in or related to their program of study or in further education.

DeKalb Technical College has two campuses and five centers conveniently located throughout DeKalb, Rockdale, Morgan and Newton Counties. The college has 264 full-time faculty and staff members and approximately 350 part-time instructors, all qualified academically as well as experientially in their respective fields.

"Our mission is focused and straightforward," said DTC President Robin Hoffman. "We prepare individuals for successful employment and fulfilling careers through state-of-the-art technical education and training. We do this by providing the full scope of workforce development services, technical education, economic development, and literacy."

All total, the college, a unit of the Technical College System of Georgia and one of the oldest of the thirty-four technical colleges in the state, offers more than 120 programs of study in the fields of Business Technologies, Computer Information Systems and Engineering Technologies, Health and Human Services, and Transportation Technologies. As a degree-granting institution, DeKalb Tech is accredited by the Commission on Colleges of the Southern Association of Colleges and Schools (SACS) to award Associate of Applied Science Degrees.

DeKalb Technical College also provides programs and services for adult learners including adult basic education, GED preparation and testing, English literacy programs, and citizenship education (EL/Civics). DeKalb Tech's adult education program is, in fact, one of the largest adult and international programs in the state.

The Economic Development Division offers a host of business and industry services that enhance economic and workforce development by providing customized

contract training and services for new, existing, and expanding companies and organizations in the college's service area. In addition, DTC also offers continuing education and open-enrollment general interest classes for the community.

New to DeKalb Tech is the Career Pathways Program, a partnership program that gives high school students the opportunity to work toward a high school diploma and a Technical Certificate of Credit simultaneously.

The college also has a new Regional Transportation Center offering Commercial Truck Driver licenses (CDL Class A); MARTA Coach Driver licenses (CDL Class B); and third-party CDL testing, as well as certification for Electrical Lineworker Apprentice (ELA).

As programs continue to grow and expand, so does the need for new and improved facilities. Just this year, a monumental milestone was marked with the grand opening of Phase One of a major renovation at the college's original campus—also described by the school as "The Renaissance of the Clarkston Campus." At a cost of $25 million, the Renaissance is the first major renovation at the Clarkston campus since 1961.

Specifically, the new renovation includes a 78,000-square-foot, two-story educational facility, as well as a 20,000-square-foot state-of-the-art Conference Center. The education facility features a 15,000-square-foot Learning Resource Center, a Student Success Center, and classrooms and labs for general education, computer information systems, and business technology studies. The Conference Center features over 10,000 square feet of meeting space with flexible layout options for student activities as well as public business meetings, seminars, wedding receptions, banquets and holiday parties. A second and third phase of the Renaissance will include renovations of the existing space for Student Affairs, the creation of a "One Stop-Shop" environment, and finally the renovation, enhancement and complete upgrade of the Clarkston campus' four original facilities.

"The Renaissance at the DeKalb Technical College Clarkston Campus ushers in a new dawn with the opening of the new Academic Building and Conference Center," Dr. Hoffman said. "A modern library, additional classrooms and computer labs, and space for Student Affairs create an even richer environment for the lifelong pursuit of knowledge. The world-class Conference Center provides a viable link to the community."

In his opening remarks as the keynote speaker for the January 2008 grand opening event, Commissioner of the Technical College System of Georgia, Ron Jackson, not only emphasized the value of technical education but also applauded the college for its great accomplishments.

"Technical colleges are important to the economic viability of the state," he said. "Technical College graduates are sought after in the business community, and DeKalb Technical College is a microcosm of what must be done in technical education throughout the state of Georgia."

For more information on DeKalb Technical College, visit them on the web at www.dekalbtech.edu or call 404-297-9522.

Above: 2008 Academic Building provides the new public image for the Clarkson Campus.

Below: Commissioner of the Technical College System of Georgia, Ron Jackson, and DTC President Robin Hoffman cut the ribbon to the new Clarkson Campus facility as area and state dignitaries and College staff and students enjoy the moment.

Georgia Hispanic Chamber of Commerce

Already the largest minority group in the United States, there is no doubt that Hispanic Americans are an integral part of this great country. And as that population continues to grow, so does the need for organizations to not only support and promote domestic and international economic development of Hispanic businesses and individuals, but to also to serve as a link between non-Hispanic entities and the Hispanic market.

The Atlanta Hispanic Chamber of Commerce was founded in 1984 by a group of dedicated leaders as they realized the enormous potential of the U.S. Hispanic business community and the need for a local organization to represent their interests and fulfill their needs through the public and private sector.

In 2000 the Georgia Hispanic Chamber of Commerce (GHCC) took the name it holds today in an effort to broaden its scope to assist all segments of the state's Hispanic community.

"Georgia's Hispanic community is nearly 750,000 people and has a buying power of $12.4 billion. The Hispanic population is growing more rapidly than the total population, a trend that is projected to continue. Additionally, there are about 20,000 Hispanic-owned businesses, and Hispanics' economic clout will rise to slightly

over $1.2 trillion in 2012," said GHCC President and CEO Sara Gonzalez. "I believe these numbers speak volumes about the contributions of Hispanics to our state and our nation. Our job at GHCC is to herald these contributions and to continue to advance this growing potential."

At the chamber's helm since 1996, Gonzalez says that the GHCC offers valuable resources such as business referrals, business expos, membership discounts, job bank access, an awards gala and many networking opportunities to its nearly 1,000 members.

Gonzalez is especially proud of the Hispanic American Center for Economic Development (HACED), which was founded in 2001 as the educational arm of GHCC with the objective of advancing the formation and growth of Hispanic businesses in Georgia. The goal of the HACED Business Incubator is to nurture start-ups and emerging businesses during the early stage of development when they are most at risk. HACED reduces business failure by providing the chosen client companies with the necessary tools to be successful during those critical early years.

"We are very pleased with the success of HACED. In fact, in 2006 alone, a total of 161 new businesses were started and, according to economists, created $44 million in new wealth for the state," she said.

Gonzalez further said that HACED has been working on expanding its educational programs throughout the state by opening satellite offices.

For more information on the GHCC, call 404-929-9998 or visit www.ghcc.org. For more information on HACED, call 770-457-6770 or visit www.haced.org.

Huddle House

When high school football fans in the close-knit community of Decatur started looking for a warm inviting place to "huddle up" with family and friends after Friday night games, little did they know that their simple need would be the inspiration for a highly successful corporation still popular and growing after more than four decades.

Little did they know that this twenty-four hour neighborhood diner—opened just for them in April 1964 by local resident John Sparks and appropriately named Huddle House by his wife—would in just two years be actively franchised, with restaurants popping up in communities throughout Georgia and the United States. Today, in fact, this Atlanta-based corporation and family restaurant franchise has more than 430 stores in seventeen states throughout the southeast, Missouri and mid-Atlantic regions, with additional new development areas in the mid-west and southwestern United States.

And, it all started in DeKalb County. "We are so proud to be a part of DeKalb County's rich history, and to have this wonderful community be such an integral part of our own company history," said Phil Greifeld, CEO of Huddle House, Inc. "I can't think of a better place to call home."

Though driven by a winning recipe for success since the beginning, Huddle House constantly endeavors to enhance its already positive image as a popular neighborhood diner where hungry people can gather with good friends to enjoy delicious, cooked-to-order meals seasoned with plenty of southern hospitality. It was just a few years ago, in fact, that Huddle House completely updated its image, building new restaurants modeled on colorful diners from the 1950s, freshening its logo and employee uniforms, and designing a new menu to relate to a broader taste while still staying true to the original favorites. New menu offerings such as the "Big House" breakfast and sandwich platters, lunchtime salads and USDA Choice steak dinners, have quickly become Huddle House signatures.

"Our goal is to keep getting better and to continue fulfilling our mission statement and customer pledge to deliver quality service and quality food to every customer, every day, every meal," Greifeld said.

With system-wide sales routinely topping $230 million per year and growing, and as the recipient of coveted awards such as the "Hot Again" award from the restaurant industry's primary publication, *National Restaurant News*, there is no doubt that Huddle House is fulfilling that mission and pledge.

For more information on Huddle House or to discover the many reasons why the Huddle House brand is one of the hottest franchise concepts in the industry, call 1-800-418-9555 or visit www.huddlehouse.com.

✧

Above: Big House Breakfast platter.

Below: The Huddle Burger with bacon.

FOX 5 Atlanta WAGA

WAGA...is Atlanta, Georgia. Like the city it proudly serves for nearly six decades, WAGA-TV has grown, prospered, and continues to set the standard for local news, information and entertainment.

The year was 1949, and the beginnings were humble: a small two story house on Peachtree Street, where the kitchen doubled as a control room. Soon the fledgling CBS affiliate was moving into bigger digs in 1951 and, in 1966, inaugurated its current home as "The Television Center of The South" on twenty-eight sprawling acres, once a home to the Creek Indians and later trod upon by U.S. Army General W. T. Sherman. It is on this historic ground, WAGA continues to document history every day.

Atlantans saw their city, nation and world unfold through the eyes of WAGA: from "I Love Lucy" to Walter Cronkite, the first game of the Atlanta Falcons to the first trip our Atlanta Braves made to the World Series. Whether it was *Who Shot JR?*, the annual running of the Peachtree Road Race or the annual MLK Memorial Services, Georgians came together to watch Channel 5.

Through the decades, WAGA has not just informed...but innovated. It was the first station in the nation to provide daily editorials, brought viewers the first hour-long newscast in 1973, a full-time investigative unit in 1977, the debut of the locally-produced nightly "PM Magazine" in 1978, and in 1992 reinvented morning television with the premiere of "Good Day Atlanta." WAGA continues to be one of the country's most respected news organizations, delivering more locally produced news and information than any other station.

In 1994 it was WAGA who shook up the television landscape with a groundbreaking affiliation with television's most innovative network, FOX. This move allowed WAGA to not only dramatically expand its commitment to local news and information, while partnering with a network that thrives on challenge and change.

WAGA, now FOX 5 Atlanta, continues to be one of the most watched FOX Stations in America, bringing viewers such favorites as "24", "House" and the number one show on television, "American Idol." FOX 5's 10 pm News is among the top ranked prime time newscasts in the nation, and the station has received numerous honors including the Peabody award, countless Emmys, and the Georgia Association of Broadcasters Station of the Year.

"It all comes down to three words," said Vice President/General Manager Gene McHugh. "Dedicated. Determined. Dependable. It's our motto, our legacy...our daily goal. Whether it's on Channel 5 or now online at myfoxatlanta.com, our mission remains the same as it was when we started in the little house on Peachtree: know, respect and serve our viewer. We are Atlanta Georgia, Atlanta Georgia...depends on us."

For more information, visit the station's website www.myfoxatlanta.com.

Above: FOX 5 Atlanta's new studio.

Below: FOX 5 Atlanta is located at 1551 Briarcliff Road Northeast in Atlanta, Georgia.

Leadership DeKalb

"We Put Unity in Community," is the slogan which reflects one of Leadership DeKalb's major goals.

Founded by the DeKalb Chamber of Commerce in 1986 to educate DeKalb's corporate leadership about the problems and opportunities they were facing as the county was growing, the organization has focused on bringing together diverse leaders to help move the county forward.

As the program grew in size, Leadership DeKalb became an independent nonprofit organization in 1994. Continuing the goals of getting leaders from varying backgrounds and professions to work together, the organization has grown to over 850 graduates. Each year, a class of forty-five to fifty people is introduced to a wide range of issues facing the county.

The ten-month curriculum includes a thought-provoking mix of program days including our county history, government, education, health, economic development, public safety and justice, as well as nuts and bolts experiences like riding a shift with a police officer and attending governmental meetings and budget hearings.

Many graduates attribute the Leadership DeKalb experience with giving them the connections and encouragement to move into higher levels of public service through their jobs and personal lives as well as running for public office. The program features a look at the county not available anywhere else.

As the organization grows, more and more companies become sponsors and active members in the leadership of the organization. Leadership DeKalb focuses on connecting its members with each other and the community. A concerted effort is made to have the members of each class be reflective of the county's rich cultural and ethnically diverse population.

In 1988, members created Youth Leadership DeKalb, a program designed for high school students to learn about community, diversity, team building, economic issues, politics, education, and personal leadership. Participants are chosen from DeKalb students who show the qualities of an emerging leader.

This program has graduated over 350 students, many of whom have returned to the DeKalb community and launched rewarding careers.

Leadership DeKalb collaborates with other organizations to create events of interest to the community, including political forums and our popular Eggs & Issues Breakfasts where the public is invited to join us. As a non-partisan organization, Leadership DeKalb welcomes conversations of importance to the well-being and future of the county and the metro region. The organization enters its third decade of community leadership training with an emphasis on bringing the many ethnic and cultural groups closer together as we create a viable and healthy region and a better place for our children and their children.

Above: The Class of 2006 was the twentieth class to graduate from the Leadership DeKalb training program. The organization has over 850 graduates.

Below: Each year, the new class begins the program with an orientation of what to expect during the ten-month training program. Leadership DeKalb CEO Vernon Jones addresses the Class of 2007.

Northwoods Montessori

The desire to provide an educational program for children of diverse backgrounds led Joanna Holland and Beth Samples to found Montessori World of Children in Decatur in 1972. As the school expanded to a second location in Doraville, the name changed to Northwoods Montessori.

Affiliated with Association Montessori International (A.M.I.) since its inception, Northwoods provides multi-age, ungraded classrooms for more than 250 children from twelve months to twelve years of age. All faculty hold an A.M.I. certificate for the level at which they teach and longevity of the faculty is characteristic.

The Montessori approach is a unique complex of philosophy, psychology, educational theory and instructional material, guided by an understanding of developmental stages and respect for individual characteristics. The classroom allows children to learn independently in an environment especially prepared to respond to the needs and tendencies of each developmental level. The school's stated purpose is to provide a foundation for lifelong learning which enhances personal integration and understanding of interdependence.

In 1994, Northwoods implemented the first All Day Montessori program in the Southeast. Through this program, the Montessori approach is used not just in the morning, but throughout the day, incorporating lunch and nap time as well as gardening, cooking and other "real life" activities. The first A.M.I. Montessori Toddler Community in the metro Atlanta area was established here in 2002.

Proud of their community, students and staff have participated in numerous community service projects over the years such as the Atlanta Community Food Bank, Our House and Habitat for Humanity. An annual Peace Celebration to honor Dr. Martin Luther King, Jr., and other peacemakers is held each January where students express in word and song the work done in the school's peaceful classrooms every day.

Proud of their school, alumni often return after they graduate high school and college to share their stories and visit. A recently-formed alumni group seeks to help these and all former students reconnect and offer them an opportunity to give back to the school. It is especially delightful when the child of a former student is enrolled.

"Life-long learning is a reality for all of us fortunate enough to teach and study at Northwoods," Samples said of the school she co-founded with Holland. "Each spring the perfume of a gardenia planted by Joanna is a sweet reminder of our roots. Our DeKalb County environs have blessed us with families from all over the world and enable us to truly be a world of children."

Visitors and those seeking enrollment for their children are always welcome to visit the school. For more information, call (770) 457-7261 or (404)284-4872 or please visit www.northwoodsmontessori.com.

M. Cary & Daughters Plumbing Contractors, Inc.

The history of M. Cary & Daughters Plumbing Contractors, Inc., is one of the county's more interesting and inspiring ones, showcasing a success story involving family unity, hard work, gender equality, and how it all came together to help fulfill an American dream.

It all began in 1978 in Brooklyn, New York when Mitchel Cary and his wife, Ronnalee, decided Atlanta and DeKalb County would be a good place for their two young daughters, Melissa and Michelle, to grow up. The area offered a "big city" atmosphere and a growing economy which appeared to be a good place to start a business.

Mitch immediately found plenty of demand for his skills as a plumber, and with Roni working as his assistant, the groundwork was laid for what would become M. Cary & Daughters. As Missi (Melissa) and Misha (Michelle) grew older, on days when Roni could not assist her husband the girls were drafted.

Missi was recruited when she was ten years old and immediately fell in love with the business. "I got to make a mess and not get in trouble for it," she laughs. Through the years she became a skilled plumber, and thus, M. Cary & Daughters was born. When she was eighteen in 1986, Missi was featured in a *Ms.* magazine article posing with a huge plumber's wrench with the caption, "I'd rather do the dirty work." Misha, two years younger, served as her assistant. Today, Michelle is office manager for the company, and Melissa works on special jobs.

Seeing that his daughters took to the job like the proverbial "ducks to water," Mitch did not hesitate to put them through the vigorous paces of the plumbing trade. "I would send them anywhere I'd send a guy," he said. "If they were going to be plumbers, I wanted them to be the best." It worked.

During the past thirty years the company has shown steady growth and gained a reputation for quality work and dependability. "We strive to provide high quality plumbing services and parts for all of our customers," Mitch emphasized.

The business, now located on busy Church Street in Decatur, offers full service plumbing, including water and sewer service replacements, renovations, repairs, remodeling, and service for any unforeseen situations connected with plumbing problems. "Over the years we have seen it all," Michelle comments, "from the sublime to the ridiculous, but we strive to do what needs to be done to serve the customers' needs and to make them happy."

M. Cary & Daughters has grown to thirteen employees. Its five big white trucks with the bold red lettering and pink tissue are common sights crisscrossing the metro area.

HAVEN TRUST BANK

Haven Trust Bank's history began nearly a decade ago when a group of Indian investors saw a need to better serve Atlanta's then small community of business entrepreneurs, especially among the area's fast-growing Asian-American businesses. While the bank originally primarily served an Indian-American clientele, today it is successfully expanding its customer base to include multicultural and mainstream communities.

"Our emphasis on customer service means going beyond just providing a loan or CD," says current CEO/President Ed Briscoe, "It means understanding our customers and their needs so we can create a special partnership. We believe this is unique for a bank these days. It enables us as well as our customers to be more efficient, more profitable, and more innovative."

The Patels—Mike, R. C., and Bobby—surveyed the local financial scene in 2000 and saw a future where a local bank serving Indian Americans would be a success. Dr. Sumant "Doc" Kapoor, Tony Patel, Danny Patel, Bill Patel and Brij Kapoor joined the effort and Horizon Bank was born. The name was later changed to Haven Trust Bank to avoid confusion when an out of state bank with a similar name expanded into the metro Atlanta area.

In 2004 the bank's headquarters was moved to its current location at Sugarloaf Parkway in the rapidly growing area now called Gwinnett Center. To reaffirm its commitment to the DeKalb County community, the bank acquired a site at Lawrenceville Highway and North Druid Hills Road where today it has its largest office with more than $100 million in deposits. Besides the company headquarters at Sugarloaf and the Decatur office, other branches are strategically located in Johns Creek and in Snellville.

During its short history, Haven Trust has seen rapid, but steady growth. Beginning with only seven employees, it has grown to a staff of over seventy.

Haven Trust Bank's total assets as of December 31, 2007, were $505 million, a thirty-five percent increase from December 31, 2006. As of December 31, 2007, loan totals were $421 million, deposit totals were $426 million and net income for the year end was $5.985 million. Looking to the future, the bank plans continued growth in the Metro Atlanta market.

The bank's board of directors, management, and employees are involved in the civic and charitable activities of the communities they serve. Among the many organizations with which Haven Trust is involved are the Gwinnett County Chamber of Commerce, the DeKalb County Chamber of Commerce, the North Fulton Chamber of Commerce, the Johns Creek Chamber of Commerce, the Council for Quality Growth, March of Dimes, American Cancer Society, BAPS (Swaminarayan Hindu Temple), Gwinnett Children's Shelter, and Women's Legacy of Gwinnett.

✧

Above: CEO Ed Briscoe.

Below: Haven Trust Bank's headquarters in Sugarloaf.

WILLIAMS, TURNER & MATHIS, INC.

The Williams family name and the independent insurance agency business are synonymous with DeKalb's recent history. As the dynamic, prosperous 1960s in the county came to a close, Raymond S. Williams, Jr., had spent years as a top agent. In 1970 he decided it was time to establish his own agency. It opened with two employees on Montreal Road in Tucker next to the same location where its successor Williams, Turner & Mathis operates today.

Today, Williams, Turner & Mathis, Inc. has twenty-four employees and is a high-tech operation, using the latest computer technology. The company currently serves more than 2,500 clients, both personal and business, and its premiums exceed $14 million a year.

The agency has always been a family affair. When he opened the business, Ray, Jr.'s wife, Helen, was co-owner and office manager. His son, Ray III, who is now chief executive officer, began working with his father when he was a student at Georgia State University and has been with the firm since 1972. Lynn, his daughter, began work with the company when she was a teenager, and, after graduating from the University of Georgia in 1978, she went to work full time shortly after the sudden and untimely death of Ray, Jr., from a heart attack in 1977.

As the company was recovering from its founder's passing, Helen was elected president and Ray III was named secretary-treasurer. With the arrival of Lynn, the family united to carry forward Ray, Jr.'s, vision of what a strong independent agency should be.

"Besides our outstanding insurance company relations, we would not be where we are today if we had not been blessed with outstanding employees. Every small business has its share of employee turnover; however, we have an unusual number of long term employees" reflects Ray.

In 1995 a major event in the company's history occurred when the Raymond S. Williams Agency merged with the local firm, Farmer, Heinz, Smither and Turner. Out of that merger came Williams, Turner & Mathis, Inc.

Ray has served as chair of the Young Agents Committee of Georgia and president of the DeKalb Association of Independent Agents. He is married to the former Sue Ellen Owens. They have four children and three grandchildren.

Lynn has served as chair of the Young Agents Committee of Georgia, chair of the National Young Agents Committee for the Independent Agents of America and was the first woman president of the Independent Agents of Georgia. She and her husband, Russell, have two children.

Above: The outstanding staff at Williams, Turner & Mathis, Inc.

Below: Lynn Mathis, Helen Williams, and Ray Williams, III, stand with rendering of Ray Williams, Jr.

R. L. Brown & Associates, Inc.

For nearly a quarter of a century, R. L. Brown & Associates, Inc. (RLB), a highly recognized and respected architectural firm located in downtown Decatur, has been "Building Communities by Design™"—one blueprint, one design, one award-winning project at a time.

Founded in 1984 by Robert L. Brown, Jr., FAIA, the firm's president and chief executive officer is a fellow of the American Institute of Architects, a designation which fewer than two percent of all registered architects in the United States hold. Although his mother was a seamstress and his father a builder, as a child Robert dreamed of becoming an architect even though none existed in his small community, making his accomplishment especially profound. Today, Barbara Willis-Brown is HR director and their son Robert L. Brown is director of finance; daughter Robyn Denise Brown attends high school in Decatur.

Today, Robert's dreams have been realized through his work illustrating the vision of designing communities where people can learn, live, work and play. His objectives are evident in the design of elementary and middle school prototypes such as Bethune Middle School, and Middle Grove High School, among others, where children learn.

Demonstrations of project diversity at educational facilities include the National Center for Bioethics in Research & Healthcare at Tuskegee University, Camille Cosby Center at Spelman College, the Student Center at Clark Atlanta University, Morehouse College Leadership Center and The Ray Charles Performing Arts Center as well as the Academic Center at Georgia Perimeter College in Dunwoody. Library prototypes designed by the firm include the William C. Brown Wesley Chapel and Covington/Flat Shoals Library.

Other projects have included Beulah Baptist and St. Phillip A.M.E. Church, where people praise, and the Olympic Tennis Venue at Stone Mountain, Butler Street YMCA and Gresham Recreation Center, where people play.

Indeed, over the years, RLB has made significant contributions in helping to shape the county as he once aspired in his youth. Anyone who has been in DeKalb County or Metro Atlanta, has probably visited, worked or continued their education in a facility planned and designed by RLB.

Utilizing a collaborative team approach to creatively and effectively meet and exceed client expectations. RLB employs a veteran staff of talented architects, planners, interior designers, project managers, construction contract administrators and support professionals.

RLB is proud of their record of professional accomplishments, as well as their impressive list of clients; Coca-Cola, Sears, Delta Airlines, Hartsfield-Jackson International Airport, and Emory University are just a few that round out the firm's impressive growth and depth of design services.

Some of the firm's most notable projects include the Birmingham Civil Rights Institute, Grand Overlook at the Atlanta History Center, MARTA Medical Center Rapid Transit Station, and Atlanta Hawks/Phillips Arena Parking Deck.

For more information on R. L. Brown & Associates, visit www.rlbrown.com or call 404-377-2460.

✧

Below: Morehouse College Leadership Center.

Bottom, right: Robert L. Brown, Jr., FAIA.

Antioch-Lithonia Baptist Church

Established shortly after the Civil War in 1867, DeKalb's Antioch–Lithonia Missionary Baptist Church is most likely the county's oldest church and most certainly has one of its richest histories. Founded with twelve faithful members who spent $2.50 to build a brush arbor for worship, the church now holds services in a state-of-the art $6.2 million sanctuary, uniquely called a "Worshiptorium" by Pastor James C. Ward. It has enough hi-tech equipment to produce hi-definition television programs and Broadway style musical productions.

A talented musician who plays several instruments, Pastor Ward said, "Sometimes people say I'm a musician masquerading as a minister." He has guided the church since 1995 and is known for his erudite, Bible-based, Christ-centered sermons which reflect his highly educated background. Pastor Ward has a Bachelor of Science in accounting from the University of New Orleans, a Masters of Divinity from the New Orleans Baptist Seminary, and he also earned a bachelor's degree from Atlanta's Morehouse College, where he was a member of its renowned Glee Club, with a double major in philosophy and German literature and a minor in music.

Commenting on Antioch's mission and vision Pastor Ward said, "Our members are individuals who want to belong to a progressive church with all of the modern programs and amenities, but yet with the warmth of the personal touch. We serve people who desire diversity in worship style; therefore, our choirs perform contemporary and traditional gospel songs, classical anthems, metered hymns, sacred harp note singing, and gospel hip-hop. We operate 'in the Spirit' and minister with a spirit of excellence."

From its modest beginning, Antioch has grown steadily, and in 1872, under the leadership of Reverend John C. Center, purchased three acres in the Lithonia vicinity for $150 and built a structure valued at $800.

The church reached a milestone in 1911 when a new stone structure, which served the congregation until recently, was erected. This sturdy structure, which was purchased by a sister congregation, is still a Lithonia landmark.

Under Pastor Ward's leadership the congregation purchased twenty-three acres on Rock Chapel Road and completed the present edifice in 2004, which was the first phase of a strategic building program. Included in the program are plans for a Family Life Center and a home for senior citizens.

Antioch now has more than 3500 members. In Pastor Ward's first year, a Marketing Ministry was organized and established to make the church more visible in DeKalb and metro Atlanta.

Speaking of the church's rich past and promising future, Pastor Ward commented, "As a congregation with a rich history and heritage we seek to preserve the past, perform in the present, and prepare for the future. We believe making history is just as important as studying history. We possess memories and vision. Although we are in an exciting new era, we must never forget our historical roots," he concludes.

Above: Antioch-Lithonia Baptist Church is located at 2152 Rock Chapel Road in Lithonia and on the Internet at www.antiochlithonia.org.

Below: Frontal view as seen from Highway 124 (Turner Hill Road) with Pastor James C. and First Lady Idell Ward superimposed.

Gerald Carter Construction Company, Inc.

Gerald Carter, founder and owner of Gerald Carter Construction Company, Inc.

Gerald Carter began working in construction when he was eighteen years old in 1956, and two years later founded the first successful general contracting company in DeKalb County owned and operated by an African American.

Carter was prompted to start his own company when, after working for two years with his first employer; he was turned down for what he considered a much deserved raise.

A fast learner, he recalls, "After two years I felt like I had learned how to do the work," and more importantly, he emphasized, "I learned how to do the billing and invoices." Thus, Gerald Carter Construction Company, Inc., was born.

Carter Construction, mainly using various subcontractors for both residential and commercial work and using the skills its founder and owner had learned from his first and only job working for others, got off to a successful beginning and showed steady progress over the years, reaching a milestone in 1984 when the company had its first million dollar year.

An example of Carter's early business savvy occurred three years after he began the business when the man he had originally worked for called for help on some jobs. "I never thought I would hear him say this," Carter remembers, when his old boss told him that he had a much better operation than his. Carter Construction was automated and used less than half the workforce of his former employer. In the early seventies before cell phones were in vogue, Carter Construction was using mobile phones in the business.

From the late 50s, shortly after its founding, on into the 60s, 70s, and 80s, Carter Construction grew incrementally, doing jobs not only in DeKalb, but throughout metro Atlanta and as far away as West Virginia.

Over the years Carter Construction has been involved in building apartments, condominiums, office buildings, and residential subdivisions. In 1985, shortly after the company hit the million dollar gross sales mark, it developed DeKalb's upscale Hunter Valley subdivision.

In the mid-1970s when there was a marked slowdown in local construction work, Carter Construction showed its versatility when it took the opportunity to help with residential development in West Virginia.

Primarily a general contracting firm, Carter Construction employs numerous local subcontractors rather than maintain a large staff. National building behemoths such as A.G. Spanos and Crow, Pope and Carter were counted among the company's clients. At one time Carter Construction did the majority of the work for the Blonder Development firm, at the time one of metro Atlanta's top builders.

Although semi-retired, Carter still does occasional select jobs "when the price is right."

City of Chamblee

"Chamblee is a community in constant motion, with a multitude of languages and a desire to always learn more about the ever-changing world. With award-winning schools, community based services, multi-modal transportation access, adjacency to the metropolitan Atlanta markets, major employment centers, and a wide variety of housing opportunities, Chamblee has many positive opportunities to build upon....." Chamblee Community Vision.

As Chamblee celebrates its centennial it looks back on a history where dairies, railroads, the military, and industrial development played large roles in its formation. While the city moves into the twenty-first century the history is being written in a multitude of languages as it becomes a true international city with a more ethnically diverse population than any municipality in the Southeast.

Early in Chamblee's history the Norfolk and Roswell Railroad formed the junction where the city is located, which later aided the progress of the many dairies which dotted the rolling hills around the town. In 1917 during WWI a new military installation named Camp Gordon was built in the heart of the city making Chamblee a boom town with many new and varied businesses.

After WWII the city experienced growth in its industrial areas, largely based on the opening of a General Motors plant in the nearby city of Doraville. Other large corporations such as Frito-Lay, Kodak, and General Electric built plants along a newly constructed Peachtree Industrial Boulevard. They provided a strong tax base and were a source of nearly full local employment for more than three decades.

The 1980s saw some dramatic changes in local demographics as many refugees and immigrants were drawn to affordable housing available in Chamblee neighborhoods along Buford Highway. The 1990 census confirmed the demographic change in the city, and seeing the shift in population as a positive step, Chamblee City Council developed new zoning to address the special needs of a diverse community. An International Village overlay was the first zoning in metro Atlanta that allowed for mixed-use development and championed livable, pedestrian-friendly neighborhoods.

✧

City of Chamblee elected officials (from left to right) Councilman Scott Taylor, Mayor Eric Clarkson, Councilman Mark Wedge, Councilman Gary King, and Councilman Dan Zanger. Not pictured: Councilman Jim Copeland.

Beginning in 2000, Chamblee developed into a strong community that combines neighborhoods and areas of commerce. The city is adding new housing to complement existing housing, and new employment centers are enhancing its diversity. Because of its in-town location and established history, most development opportunities are in the redevelopment of obsolete industrial and heavy commercial land uses and infill on scattered vacant parcels.

Chamblee is a city proud of having high level services for all members of the community at relatively low tax rates. Each city department strives to be proactive in addressing challenges, inclusive in its decision-making and respectful of the diversity of ideas and cultures that make Chamblee the vibrant city it is today.

CHAMBLEE CITY HALL
CHAMBLEE GEORGIA

DeKalb Chamber of Commerce

Founded in 1938 with the dual mission of building a better community in which to live and work, and maintaining a sound operating climate for business and industry, the DeKalb Chamber of Commerce continues to be the driving force behind the county's development.

Above: Chamber President Leonardo McClarty speaks at the Capitol.

Below: Board Chair Patrick Putnam, Chamber President Leonardo McClarty and Congressman Hank Johnson.

The Chamber has evolved over the years mirroring the county itself, which has grown from a rural agriculture-based economy to the suburban-urban economy and culture of today.

"During the early years any size business of substance was a member of the Chamber," current President and CEO Leonardo McClarty commented. "People like the Rutlands, the Shepherds, H.G. Patillo, and Robert Lanier, Sr., to mention a few, were some of the people who played integral roles in the development of the Chamber and the county."

In the intervening years there have been many milestones in the Chamber's history and development. Beginning in the 1950s and 1960s the organization was in the forefront of some of DeKalb's most expansive commercial and industrial development. That development has continued unabated into the 2000s.

As the business and cultural needs of DeKalb have changed, the Chamber has transformed itself to meet those changing needs. "Moving forward, the Chamber will continue to advocate for business and a strong, educated workforce," McClarty emphasized. "Our goal is to make sure that DeKalb County remains a place where business can continue to thrive and find success. Education will always be supported because existing business cannot prosper and you cannot recruit quality industry without a qualified workforce."

Through a thriving and growing membership, the Chamber provides services in four main areas. It functions as a resource clearinghouse, providing technical assistance to businesses, including business planning and lending resources. The Chamber also monitors and reviews local and state legislation, often advocating on policy that is advantageous to business. Business development opportunities abound as does bottom line cost savings. Members are eligible for preferred pricing on office supplies and group insurance policies.

Chamber Board Chairman Patrick Putman reiterated, "The DeKalb Chamber has always been a key component in what makes DeKalb County great, and we will continue to promote a pro business climate so that citizens may have an unparallel quality of life."

The Chamber's most recent milestone was a relocation of its offices in 2007 from its longtime Decatur location to the Tucker-Northlake area. Office space has been expanded, and "We will now be able to better serve the community," McClarty said. "The move is about being more accessible. This is the next step in our evolution," he added.

WILSON WELDING

The history of DeKalb's Wilson Welding Services is one of a company which began in 1954 in the backyard of John R. and Charlotte Wilson. What started out as doing small local welding jobs, has since grown into a close knit family owned enterprise with an expanded business.

Family unity has been central to the continued success of the company with the four Wilson sons, Jerry R., Jack D., Johnny W., and Phillip D., playing major roles over the years. As soon as they were old enough the boys learned to weld and during the past six decades have helped Wilson Welding become a leader in its field.

It was John's reputation for honesty, hard work, and his skill as a welder that took him from welder to business owner. His wife, Charlotte, a strong supporter of her husband, was his partner in business, doing many crucial jobs while at the same time taking care of a family of four boys and two girls.

Until his untimely death of brain cancer in 2000, Jerry, the oldest son, was a mainstay of the company, working in all phases of the operation.

Jack, who worked in the field for many years, eventually moved into the company office, helping guide operations.

Johnny, as did his brothers before him, did welding in the field for many years and then moved into the office to help oversee the company's growing and important boiler operations.

Philip, the youngest son, began with the company doing mechanic work and welding before he transferred to the boiler division based in Lithonia where he worked until his retirement.

When Wilson Boiler Service was established in the early 1960s there was a need for additional employees and Bob Williams, an expert in the field, was brought in to oversee the operation. The boiler service unit expanded its customer base throughout the southeast. As evidence of the boiler service's widespread reputation, a company as far away as Brazil called on its services. Under the leadership of Johnny, the boiler division has continued to grow. A new facility was added in McDonough six years ago, and Johnny's son, Wayne, heads that company.

Today, Wilson Welding Service employs more than fifty employees and is operated by Jack's oldest son, Jack D., II, while awaiting the fourth generation of Wilson's to learn the skills of the trade.

Services and products offered include ASME certified welders, on site welding repair, commercial, residential, food service, custom fabrication, custom truck beds, metal shearing, forming, rolling, punching, handrail, pipe, height welders, in-house precision machining facilities, equipment repairs, trailers, trailer parts, steel, aluminum stainless welding, structural erection and supplier, structural handrails, stairs and landings, forklift repairs and modifications, heavy equipment repair and machining, fabrication and machining.

✧

Above: Mr. and Mrs. John R. Wilson.

Below: Wilson Welding Service, Inc., is located at 2939 Snapfinger Road in Decatur.

ARCHETYPE DEVELOPMENT GROUP

International Village, a five-hundred-thousand-square-foot modern mixed-use development on thirty acres in Chamblee including shops, restaurants, hotels, and other attractions will make DeKalb history when it opens in late 2008. It is being developed by PDK Investment Group, LLLC, which is comprised of Archetype Management Company, LLP and its managing partner, architect Charles K. Schmandt, and the Euro Atlanta Development Group, LLC, headed by Dr. Eike Jordan. Jordan has a Ph.D. in environmental economics.

The project will cost an estimated $125 million in privately invested funds and will create approximately 2700 new jobs in the area, Schmandt said. "The International Village is a unique opportunity to be a part of Chamblee's transformation from a diverse industrialized city to a truly viable international community for local citizens and visitors alike," he added.

"The heart of the project will be the activities" Schmandt enthused. The amphitheater and the public spaces within the development are designed to accommodate street festivals, weekly entertainment shows and activities, artist markets, antique shows, and events celebrating national holidays for many different countries in addition to U.S. holidays. A full-time Events Director will come on board to provide year-round activities and to coordinate events with Plaza del Sol, a Latin Village, Antique Row, and the city of Chamblee, among other entities.

Dr. Jordan said of the project, "There is excitement from every target group we talk to. This is reflected in the long list of letters of intent of future tenants." He established Euro Atlanta Development Group in 1995 and became a major investor in International Village in early 2007.

Design standards for the Village set by Schmandt will encourage buildings, landscape, and signage to have an international look and appeal. There will be a mix of one-, two-, three-, and four-story buildings, which will be offered for lease to individual owners, investment partnerships or groups. "What we really think will pull people in is scheduling monthly festivals and weekly artist markets," he said. "People will come have lunch at one of the sidewalk cafes, see what's going on, and come back in the evening for entertainment."

✧

Eike Jordan and Chuck Schmandt, principal developers of International Village.

PDK Investment said it will go to great lengths to be environmentally sound, preserving as many trees on the heavily wooded property as possible.

Schmandt, who did much of his early work in California, has been an advocate for environmentally friendly mixed-use projects for more than four decades. He is recognized for his creative work as an architect and has received numerous awards from environmental and civic groups, including several "Santa Barbara Beautiful" awards.

Schmandt and Jordan teamed together to insure the success of International Village after an original partner withdrew from the project. Jordan said he has high hopes for the project and has been successful in seeking overseas investment for the Village.

The International Village is designed to attract workers, families, visitors, and conventioneers from metro Atlanta and also the southeast, throughout the U.S., and from overseas. "When completed it will incorporate activities and businesses to make this unique development an exciting place for everyone involved." Schmandt commented.

The International Village truly will be an integral part of DeKalb's new history.

VERNON JONES

When Vernon Jones took office in 2001, he was the first African American and youngest person ever elected as chief executive officer in DeKalb County's history. Jones presides over the Board of Commission meetings and manages the day-to-day operations of the county with an annual operating budget of $2.6 billion, representing more than 700,000 citizens. He was elected in a run-off capturing sixty-three percent of the votes in 2000, and re-elected in 2004 by a fifty-four percent margin. Avoiding a run-off in 2004, he defeated six opponents, including two state representatives and an incumbent at-large county commissioner.

The Jones Administration legacy is synonymous with long-term prosperity for DeKalb County through fiscal responsibility and progressive policies. During his tenure in office, Jones is proud to have achieved dual AAA bond credit ratings from both Moody's and Standard and Poor's Investor Services—a distinction earned by only 37 out of nearly 4,000 counties in the country. This accomplishment reaffirms confidence in the county's financial management and its economic outlook under the Jones Administration.

Within his first ninety days in office, Jones spearheaded the passage of a $125 million bond referendum for acquisition and development of parks and green space. In 2005, he achieved the historic passage of three additional bond referendums totaling $230 million for land preservation, transportation improvements and libraries—a significant landmark of his administration. Demonstrating a commitment for acquisition of green space and development of parks, Jones has acquired 2,735 acres of land that equates to a seventy percent increase in County's parks and green space.

A proven visionary, Jones sought protection and received approval from the United States Congress to designate Arabia Mountain as a National Heritage Area. Arabia Mountain, situated in the historic Klondike Community, is now a national tourist destination, listed as one of only thirty-seven national heritage areas designated by the National Park Service. It protects and preserves the granite outcrop ecosystems, wetland, pine and oak forests; as well as federally-protected plant species.

Vernon Jones was the first African American in the history of DeKalb to be elected chief executive officer.

Moreover, in 2005, the CEO launched a curbside recycling program. The first of its kind in DeKalb County, the recycling program is a proven success for voluntary participants. Some sixteen thousand citizens volunteer for the program, with participation steadily increasing.

Capital projects are major landmarks under the Jones Administration. Over the course of his administration, $800 million has been allocated for infrastructure and capital projects. These projects include major street resurfacing, sidewalks, intersection improvements and bridge repairs.

Born on October 31, 1960, Jones grew up humbly in rural Laurel Hill, North Carolina. He graduated from North Carolina Central University in Durham, earning a bachelor's degree in business administration. His public service includes eight years as a member of the Georgia House of Representatives, where his vision and leadership played a pivotal role on several key committees, including the powerful appropriations and insurance committees. His private sector experience includes leadership positions at MCI WorldCom and BellSouth Cellular.

Allied Holdings

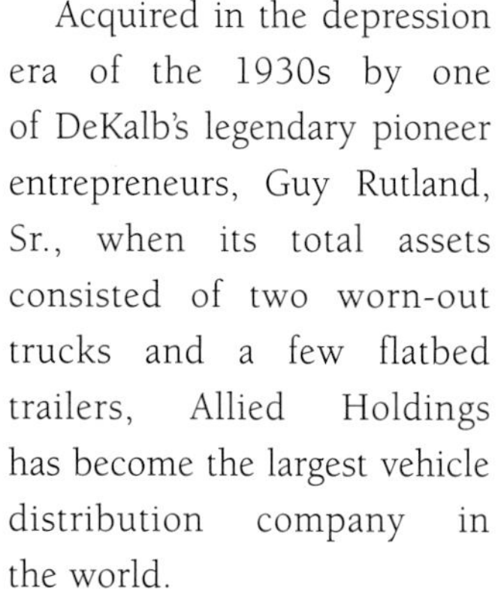

Acquired in the depression era of the 1930s by one of DeKalb's legendary pioneer entrepreneurs, Guy Rutland, Sr., when its total assets consisted of two worn-out trucks and a few flatbed trailers, Allied Holdings has become the largest vehicle distribution company in the world.

The firm's foundation is built on a combination of sound business practices and strong religious principles, which stress integrity, honesty, and ethical standards with an emphasis on caring for employees and their families. As an example, Allied Holdings is one of the few companies of its size in the nation which has a chaplaincy program for personalized ministry to its employees. The program was an outgrowth of the strong religious commitment of the Rutland family and the belief the foundation of the company be based on Christian values. "With Christian values being the foundation on which Allied conducts business and our guide in the way we relate to employees, a chaplain program seemed a natural fit," said Robert J. "Bob" Rutland, a third generation member of the family and a long time principal in the company.

Above: Guy Rutland, Jr., Guy Rutland, II, and Bob Rutland.

It was 1934 when Guy Rutland, Jr., Guy, Sr.'s oldest son and Bob's father, a recent graduate of Georgia Tech, joined what was then The Motor Convoy company and began its modernization. Using his engineering skills he quickly developed what was then a revolutionary concept in the car-hauling business, a two-deck carrier that included one over the cab of the truck. He immediately upgraded the fleet, and by 1941 The Motor Convoy had grown from two rigs to fifty-five rigs and was on its way to national prominence, hauling vehicles for most of the major American auto manufacturers.

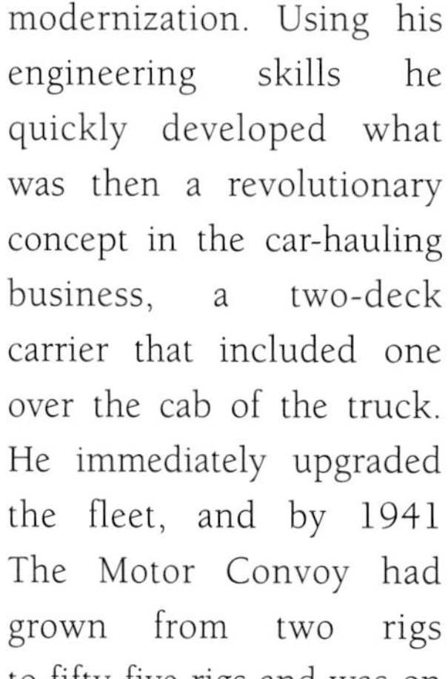

In the ensuing years, the company showed strong steady growth by acquiring other customers and shippers. Upon his graduation from the Citadel in 1961, Guy, III, oldest son of Guy, Jr., joined the company, and working closely with his father, grew The Motor Convoy exponentially. In 1964, Guy, Jr., suffered a stroke, and Guy, III, with Bob, who was attending Clemson University, assumed leadership of the company.

After having offices in various locations in DeKalb, in 1983 the company built and moved to its present location in Decatur's Fidelity Bank building.

Two milestones were reached in 1993 when Allied Holdings, Inc., was formed as the parent of Allied Systems and other subsidiaries, and the company's stock was traded on the NASDAQ Stock Exchange.

Allied Holdings, Inc., moved to the New York Stock Exchange in 1998 and to the American Stock Exchange in 2001.

The Rutland family and Allied is synonymous, where values such as family, faith, citizenship, and business ethics have been passed down for generations. Guy III presently serves as chairman emeritus. Bob, now retired, was most recently Chairman of the board after serving as CEO. Guy, IV, is senior vice president and a member of the board of directors.

CDC Federal Credit Union

Founded on March 1, 1949, in Atlanta, Georgia, CDC Federal Credit Union (CDC FCU) was chartered exclusively for the Centers for Disease Control and Prevention employees. On January 18, 1950, seven officers were elected to the board of directors, while assets of the credit union were just over $13,000 with only 263 members. Over the span of 59 years, CDC FCU has grown with assets exceeding $160 million and membership of over 16,000!

Today, the member base eligible to join and receive the many services and products of the organization includes anyone who lives, works, worships, attends school, or volunteers in portions of DeKalb, Fulton, and Gwinnett Counties. The credit union relocated its headquarters in 2006 to the Northlake Office Park area to better serve the North Atlanta Community. A grand opening celebration was hosted in early October for approximately two hundred distinguished guests, community leaders, local area business leaders and members.

"Our goal is to promote the present and future financial well-being of our members and their communities by delivering innovative products and exceptional services," said Betsy Mercier, president and CEO.

In recent years, CDC FCU has come to be recognized for its superior level of service. Among those services and products, CDC FCU offers a variety of checking and savings options including Simply Checking, Choice Checking, Student Checking, Vintage Checking and Vista Checking. All checking account features include nationwide ATM access, unlimited check writing, free Internet Banking and voice response service, overdraft protection and special rate discounts on consumer loans. Savings options include prime share savings, custom share savings, and Christmas Club accounts. Savings accounts require an initial deposit of $25, and include features such as dividends earned on monthly balances, money transfers between accounts, overdraft protection, and payroll deduction.

Other important CDC FCU services include money market accounts, certificate accounts, CUNA Mutual Investment Services and Briarwood Financial Services, LLC, which offers different features on mortgages including fixed rates, adjustable rates, second mortgages and First-Time Homebuyer Programs. Visit www.cdcfcu.com for more information on all CDC FCU products and services.

CDC FCU's main goal and future plans include community reinvestment, volunteering with charitable organizations, expanding our Select Employee Groups (SEG's), and marketing through different facets of media. One example of how CDC FCU exemplifies community involvement is through a branded program called Because We Care. This community based outreach program provides opportunities for volunteers to assist with special projects in the North Atlanta area, specifically CDC FCU's home base, DeKalb County.

"We look eagerly to our future, remaining steadfast in our commitment to maintain a superior level or service, while offering the best financial products available, and providing meaningful support to our community," said Mercier.

THOMAS E. BROWN

✧

Above: DeKalb Fire Chief Thomas Brown was one of the youngest to head a fire department of any major city or county in the nation's history.

Below: DeKalb Sheriff Thomas Brown ran unopposed in 2004 and is now serving his second term.

DeKalb County Sheriff Thomas E. Brown's meteoric rise to top positions in county government began in 1985 when he was thirty-one and named DeKalb's fire chief, making him at the time the youngest head of a fire department of any major city or county in the nation. Being elected sheriff in 2001 by an overwhelming margin was the culmination of a career during which he served as the county's public safety director placing him in charge of all public safety functions in DeKalb.

The experience as public safety director offered him a unique platform to hone his skills as a future sheriff. As an example, during his tenure in office he introduced the concept of community-oriented policing services and he spearheaded many capital improvements, such as renovation of the public safety building at no expense to the taxpayers.

As sheriff, he is responsible for the operation of the mammoth county jail, one of the largest in the country, serving all criminal and civil warrants and, very importantly in these perilous times, security of the county courthouse. The sheriff also operates DeKalb County's major Fugitive Squad Unit, which does the ever increasing job of locating and arresting fugitives.

The sheriff's office has four basic divisions: Administrative Services, Jail Services, Court Services, and Field Services.

Administrative Services is essential to the sheriff's office commitment to fiscal responsibility and accountability and to ensuring that the technology required for efficient operations is available, properly installed, and operating efficiently.

The Jail Services Division operates the jail for the safety and security of the community while providing for a safe, humane, and secure environment for both staff and inmates.

The mission of the Court Division is to serve and protect local citizens and employees by providing safety and security for all court proceedings, including transporting inmates to court proceedings, both locally and statewide. This division also serves civil process orders generated by the courts.

The Field Services Division is a twenty-four hour, seven day-a-week operation that is the main law enforcement arm of the sheriff's office. Its mission is to promote and provide safety for local citizens and visitors by enforcing state laws and county ordinances in a fair and impartial manner; to transport inmates to and from courts, county jails, and medical facilities; and to transport mentally ill persons to treatment facilities and court hearings. The division serves criminal warrants, temporary protective orders and other orders of the courts.

Summing up one philosophy of his office Sheriff Brown commented, "As in any successful organization, investing in employees is paramount, as an organization is only as good as the people who staff it.... To improve performance and services to our constituents and provide personnel training and career path opportunities, which also boost employee morale and allow us to better serve the public, are onging initiatives."

Georgia Federal Credit Union

It all started in 1958 when founding member Vernon Carne encouraged six other DeKalb County teachers to join him in pledging $5 each to start a credit union chartered by the National Credit Union Administration.

Today, the DeKalb County Teachers Federal Credit Union and its original seven members have become a very successful not-for-profit financial cooperative known as the Georgia Federal Credit Union (GFCU) with more than 80,000 individual members, 430 member groups, 10 county school systems and 14 branch locations across Georgia.

Growth has been steady over the years. In 1974, while still the DeKalb County Teachers Federal Credit Union, a charter amendment provided a huge boost to the organization's membership when services were extended to primary and secondary public, private and parochial schools, as well as colleges and universities in DeKalb County. And, in 1983, when the name changed to Georgia Federal Credit Union, even more groups and schools came on board.

Also spurring growth have been mergers with other credit unions across the state, the most recent including the Greater Atlanta Catholic Federal Credit Union and the University Employees Federal Credit Union of Athens. As a result of these mergers, GFCU is now open to all Catholics in the Archdiocese of Atlanta as well as the faculty, staff, students, and alumni of the University of Georgia.

Competitive financial services offered by GFCU include:

- Share savings accounts,
- Christmas & Vacation Savings Clubs,
- "You Name It" savings accounts,
- Individual retirement accounts—Roth traditional, and education,
- Sterling Fund money market accounts,
- Certificates of deposit,
- Checking accounts with identity theft 911 protection,
- Super Saver Kids Club,
- CU Succeed Teen Club,
- CU College Club,
- Upper Class Account for members over fifty-five,
- ATM & Visa check cards,
- Direct deposit/payroll deduction,

- E-Branch—member care call center,
- Online PC banking,
- Bill Pay,
- VISA Gold & Platinum credit cards,
- Consumer loans,
- Mortgage loans,
- Car buying service, and
- Supplemental insurance

In addition to its mission to be its members' premier source of value-priced financial services, GFCU believes strongly in the credit union philosophy of "people helping people." The organization proudly takes an active role in assisting organizations, charities, and the communities it serves through scholarships, philanthropy, volunteerism and programs from the Christmas Wish Tree Program to a free community speakers' bureau offering programs on money management, identity theft prevention and more.

GFCU also offers its services as an employee benefit with local employers. For more information about the benefits of partnering with GFCU, visit www.gfcuonline.org or call 1-888-493-GFCU.

✧

Above: GFCU attends a Dekalb County New Teacher Orientation event. Pictured from left to right are Public Relations Coordinator Tierra Daniels; Catholic Community Coordinator Hilda Zamora; and Business Development Officer Heni Jordan (back of picture).

DeKalb History Center

The DeKalb History Center, founded sixty years ago as the DeKalb Historical Society, is the official keeper of the flame for the County's rich history and is the sponsoring organization for this official history of DeKalb County.

✧

The Old Courthouse on the Square, home of the DeKalb History Center.

The Society was organized in January 1947 "for the purpose of collecting and preserving pictures, maps, letters, family histories, historical items and records of people who live in DeKalb County and this section of Georgia which is noted for its fine homes, schools, and churches." While the History Center continues to fulfill these important functions it has the added and most important responsibility of being the official custodian of the old DeKalb Courthouse, which is the focal point of the Decatur Square and is considered an historical gem.

"We have officially been located in the courthouse since 1968" Executive Director Melissa Forgey points out, "and being stewards of the county's most historic building is a responsibility we take seriously and look forward to continuing in the future."

An equally important responsibility of the Center is maintaining and displaying the Historic Complex located at 720 West Trinity Place in Adair Park. The complex includes the Historic Swanton House, Decatur's oldest town home dating to 1840, the Biffle Cabin, a log structure also dating to the mid-1800s, and is used today for craft and cooking displays, and the most recent acquisition, the Thomas-Barber Cabin, is still undergoing restoration.

The Center's Heritage education program for students is one of its favorite programs, and a Heritage Festival is held each year at the Historic Complex.

"We have a good Heritage Festival which we plan to build on," Forgey said. "The program is geared toward fifth graders from throughout the county, and we plan to expand it an additional day to allow the general public to participate in the 'hands-on' learning of our history."

The archives, located in the Courthouse and maintained by archivist Paul Graham, are used frequently by individuals and groups. Among the many historical items found there are bound volumes of the *DeKalb New Era* and *Decatur-DeKalb News-Era,* former legal organs of the county.

"The energy of sixty years of work by volunteers has gotten us where we are today," Forgey commented. She also stressed the cooperation from the county government as an important part of the Center's success.

Milestones of the Center during the past sixty years are too numerous to name in this brief history, but some of special note include the year 1965 when the Historical Society was chartered and the first by-laws written; 1969 was the move to the Courthouse and a reading room and exhibit spaces were established; 1981, additional rooms in the west wing of the Courthouse were made available to expand the exhibits into a full museum, which opened with a public ceremony and parade; 1990 the Historical Society became the official caretaker of DeKalb's Old Courthouse; 1994, grand opening of the Visitors Center celebrating partnership of DCVB and the Society; 1997, Historical Society celebrating its fiftieth year, and in 1999 the Society held its first History Camp in the summer in partnership with the Decatur-DeKalb YMCA.

The many names of those who have made major contributions over the years to the History Center are listed elsewhere in this book.

DeCuir Gourmet Company, Inc.

DeCuir Gourmet Company, Inc., formerly DeCuir Catering, is the brainchild and vision of David T. DeCuir. This endeavor did not begin as a business venture; instead, it started out of a strong desire to have every palate share in the awesome flavors of good Cajun cuisine. Although the idea was to parlay the frequent requests from friends for Cajun cooked meals into a business some day, there were no plans for that "some day" to be so soon. On July 18, 2000, the state of Georgia issued a Certificate of Incorporation for the company.

Since its inception, it has been "full steam ahead" for this fledgling enterprise. With no working capital, but a strong conviction and great expectations, David poured his paychecks and efforts into DeCuir Gourmet while still maintaining full-time employment. Friends and family have contributed greatly, and a tremendous blessing from the Lord has kept faith, business and expectations very high. Through word of mouth, DeCuir's client list is growing exponentially and the company is on the verge of becoming another great American success story.

To visualize why DeCuir Gourmet has and will prosper, it is important to understand the passions and background of its founder.

David DeCuir is the creative force behind the venture. Born and raised in Baton Rouge, Louisiana, David is passionate about maintaining his French Creole roots and sharing it through a wonderful cuisine that is uniquely American. David is a graduate of Northwestern University in Louisiana where he received a bachelor's degree in marketing. He has an abiding faith in the Creator and is fearless in his determination that success can be achieved through hard work, excellent customer service and richly seasoned Cajun food. David has worked in sales for over eleven years and brings a wealth of people skills to the table. He is an innovator and believes strongly that the "customer truly comes first." Cooking is a tradition in David's large family. He adds his own blends and flavors to the growing menu selections presented by DeCuir Gourmet.

The depth of David's creative talents and professional skill set are the key ingredients in the success of the company thus far. Armed with superb interpersonal skills, sales and marketing savvy, visual design, interior decorating skills and, of course, his mastery of culinary arts, David is poised for even greater success. His credo: "We act like a small business, but think like a big business."

He is earnest in his drive to carve out a significant place for DeCuir Gourmet in the very competitive catering industry. David's goal for DeCuir Gourmet is evidenced in his carefully thought-out mission statement. He sees success as being measured by the company's ability to create meaningful employment for others, proven partnerships with other small businesses as well as play an active role in guiding and educating young people through philanthropic endeavors and to ultimately achieve financial freedom.

For more information, call 770-982-2055 or visit www.decuircatering.com.

DeCuir Gourmet specializes in exquisite cuisine and elegant presentations.

RUTLAND CONTRACTING COMPANY

Rutland Contracting Company, ranked among DeKalb's oldest businesses, has a rich history, which began in 1919 when founder Guy W. Rutland, Sr., one of the county's first and most innovative entrepreneurs, used two mules pulling an old fashioned "scraper" to move dirt for highway and other construction projects. Today the fourth generation of his family, including two great grandsons, continues in his footsteps, using the most modern equipment and technology to carry on the Rutland legacy.

Above: This vintage Loraine shovel loads dump truck on a Rutland Contracting job in early days.

Below: Rutland Contracting Company headquarters on Atlanta Avenue in Decatur, c. the 1930s.

Rutland, Sr., who in his later years was affectionately known as "Pa" by close friends and associates, was a legendary figure in local business circles. From the time in the early 1900s when he left nearby LaGrange as a young man and stopped by little Greenville, Georgia, to pick up his soon-to-be-bride, Mary Alice Williams, on the way to Decatur, he hit the ground running, "grading roads and business sites with his mule team and doing any other jobs where he thought there was money to be made," said Jimmy Smith, III, CEO and principal owner of the company. Smith is married to the former Connie Rutland, daughter of the late Calvin Rutland, "Pa's" son who ran the family business until his sudden and untimely death in 1975.

The Rutland sons, Guy, Jr., and the aforementioned Calvin, grew up following in their father's footsteps in the construction business. Both sons had successful business careers and carried on and enhanced the two principal Rutland enterprises—Rutland Contracting Company and Allied Holdings (formerly Motor Convoy).

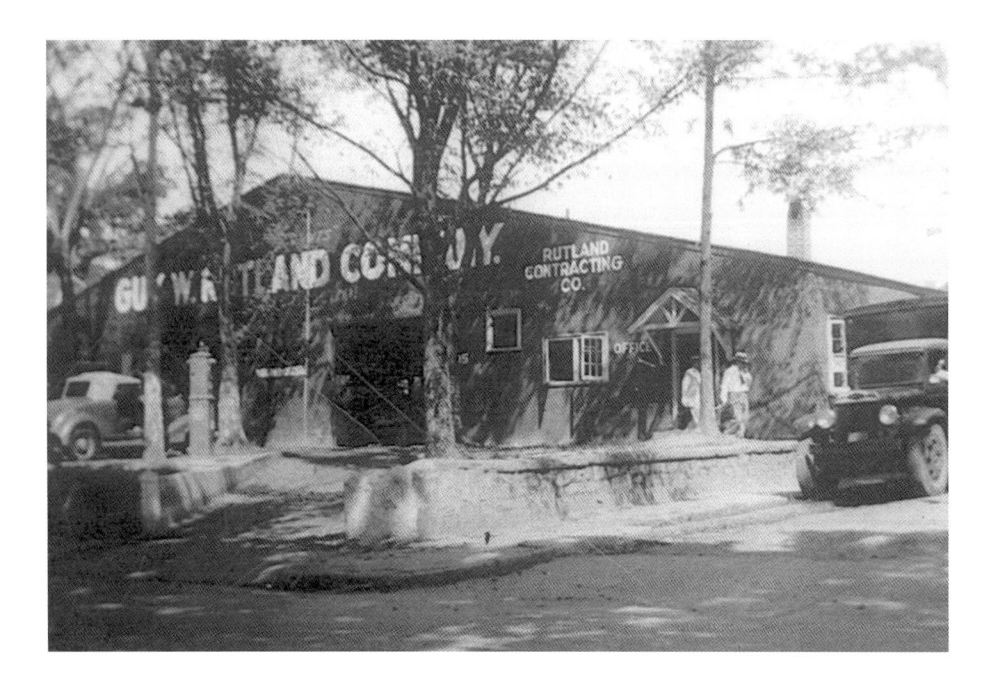

In the early days Rutland's work was concentrated on highway building in Georgia and surrounding states. During WWII, the firm contributed to the war effort by working on military bases throughout the southeast. Major projects the company has worked in the past several decades include Grady Memorial Hospital, Georgia Baptist Hospital, Mercer University, Stone Mountain Park, and Burt Adams Boy Scout Camp.

Today's Rutland Contracting Company is in the hands of the Smith family. Jimmy and his two sons, James, IV, and Robert have carried the company into the modern era. James serves as company president and Robert is secretary-treasurer.

"From the late '50s until now, we have concentrated on work in the greater Atlanta area, primarily working in the private sector," Jimmy explained. The company now mainly does site preparation for residential, industrial, shopping center, and apartment projects.

"We are proud of the history of the company and the contributions it has made to the community over the years and take great pride in the fact that there has been four generations of family in this small family owned company," Jimmy said. "And there is a James Smith, V, who may yet come into the business some time in the future and carry on the tradition."

Agnes Scott College

In her 2007 inaugural address as Agnes Scott College's eighth president, Elizabeth Kiss noted the "audacity and relevance, today as in 1889, of the college's vision of educating women for the betterment of the world."

A minister and a businessman crossed paths in Decatur and recognized the value of educating women. Believing "the proper education of a woman would influence a whole family," the Reverend Frank H. Gaines, pastor of Decatur Presbyterian Church, found an ally in church elder and businessman Colonel George Washington Scott. Papers to charter the Decatur Female Institute were filed with the Superior Court of DeKalb County July 27, 1889.

Committed to constructing the best educational building in Georgia, Colonel Scott's original $40,000 donation grew to $112,500—at that time, the largest gift ever made to education in Georgia. The school became Agnes Scott Institute in honor of his mother.

Agnes Scott is located on its original site on the south side of the Georgia Railroad; its original five acres now 100. The college's first building, Agnes Scott Hall, was built in 1891 and was lit with electricity, heated with steam and had hot and cold running water and sanitary plumbing—conveniences seldom found in college buildings before the turn of the century.

In 1906 the institute became a college, awarded its first degrees as a college and formed its student self-governed honor system, which has become a cornerstone of life at Agnes Scott. The next year, Agnes Scott became the first institution of higher education in Georgia to receive regional accreditation. In 1926 it became the second college in Georgia to hold membership in Phi Beta Kappa.

The college emphasis on academic excellence and a rigorous liberal arts curriculum "fully abreast of the best institutions of this country" has always encouraged independent thinking in an atmosphere for learning. The residential campus, prized for its aesthetic distinction and state-of-the-art facilities, has given generations of students a sense of place, purpose and responsibility.

Alumnae have distinguished themselves in medicine, science, education, ministry, the arts, law, politics, business and community service. Since the 1920s, the college has ranked in the top 10 percent of American colleges whose graduates complete Ph.D. degrees. The student body of approximately 900 includes women from approximately forty states and thirty countries, representing the diversity of the United States and the world.

Today, Agnes Scott College continues to educate women to think deeply, live honorably and engage the intellectual and social challenges of their times.

Additional information on Agnes Scott College is available on the Internet at www.agnesscott.edu.

Above: Agnes Scott Hall "Main" with Letitia Pate Evans Hall in the background, c. 2007.

Below: Agnes Scott Hall "Main," c. 1900.

SPONSORS